LITERARY POTPOURRI

Vol II Anthology #3

July, August, September
2003

Other Volumes in This Series:
Vol I
Issues #1 through #4 2002
Vol.II
Issues #1 through #2 - 2003

Edited by Beverly A. Jackson

Literary Potpourri is published quarterly by Lit Pot Press, Inc., 3909 Reche Rd. Ste. #132, Fallbrook CA 92028. This issue is made possible in part by the generous funding of Levenger, manufacturers of fine writing/reading products, and the support of the readers and writers of Literary Potpourri ezine at http://www.literarypotpourri.com on the Internet.

Subscriptions: Send subscriptions to: Literary Potpourri, 3909 Reche Road, Ste. 132, Fallbrook, Ca. 92028. Single Year US (4 issues) $30.00, Foreign $42.00; Single Issues US $10.00. Foreign $12. Price includes postage. Order form online. Back Issues available.

Submissions: Send submissions to: Literary Potpourri, 3909 Reche Road, Ste. #132, Fallbrook, CA 92028 or email to litpot@adelphia.net. Accompany all work with SASE if sent by mail. Guidelines provided on the website.

Printed by: Stride Print Services, Canada.

Literary Potpourri is a trademark of Lit Pot Press

ISBN 0-9722793-8-5

LITERARY POTPOURRI
VOLUME II   ISSUE #3

TABLE OF CONTENTS

4

THE RACE

by J.E. Jacobs

It's the first time I've gone against Bunt, either as a friend or as our leader. I climb one of the big granite blocks and spit black Tootsie Roll juice between my feet.

"We ought to set up right here," I say. Bunt shakes his head like it's a stupid idea. He's wearing his Atlanta Braves jersey and I notice again how dark his skin is. Almost brown-black like the chunks of bitter chocolate Mama uses in fudge.

"You know they'll come through here," I say.

"Too easy to get pinned down, though, Case Man," Bunt says. That's what he calls me: Case Man.

"Yeah, but we'd have the element of surprise."

"Maybe so, but I'm Captain and I say we double back."

"Well maybe I'll just assume command then." I point my BB rifle at him, even though Daddy says you don't point a gun at anything unless you aim to kill it.

The big granite blocks built into the bank of the Saluda are all that's left of the old Civil War dam. The rest long since broken off in the river and smoothed into boulders by more years than I know of rushing water. Part now of what we call the "rapids." I throw a stick in the pea-green water and watch it catch and disappear in a whirlpool. There's no better place in the summer than the riverwoods. The wet crackling sounds and the smell of dark dirt and pine, and it's like God installed air-conditioning just for us kids that have to stay outside on even the hottest days.

The forest that lowers down to the river is where we play War. Us kids from Foxfire Apartments always against the rich kids from Whitehall Acres. The woods I love, but the river itself makes me nervous. I think about water so cold and from so deep. How it was in the dark before passing under the Lake Murray Dam. I heard there were whole towns buried under all that water. Whenever someone drowns in the river, like the usual high school boy too drunk to mind the floodgate sirens, I think about the water still having too much of that darkness in it. Like it's not used to so much light or laughter or boys swimming.

Stephen White drops from a branch of a pine tree, runs over to his brother Paul and pushes him. He does that a lot: pushes his brother down on the ground or thumps him on the back of the head and for no good reason. Stephen and Paul look exactly alike but are as different as cat and dog. Stephen being the dog and Paul the cat.

Stephen says to me, "What's going on, monkey breath? It's too hot for this crap."

"Close your hole, dillweed," I say back.

Debbie is throwing rocks in the river and turns around long enough to say, "I don't know, Casey, leaders shouldn't be so ugly should they?"

"Be quiet 'fore I call the dogcatcher," I say. I wouldn't ever tell anyone, but I really do like Debbie. She's so pretty and she can do stuff as good as any boy I know. When I can do it so no one sees me, I like to watch her. I like how she wears cutoff jeans over her red bathing suit and I like her long black hair and I like her olive skin. I especially like her boobs. They're big for a girl her age.

"All right, Case," Bunt says, aggravated. "If you're gonna be a baby about it, we'll just do it your way."

"Ain't no baby," I say. "Shoot, only babies believe a colored boy could ever be captain." The thick buzzing sound of the forest is turned down, almost off, like someone closed it in a closet.

"I can't believe you said that, Casey," Debbie says, and she shakes her head like Mama does. I don't know what to say so I tell her to blow it out her backside. I don't notice right off, but Bunt has climbed on my block. He has that look.

8

I've only seen it once before. Last summer, when an older boy at the Zippy Mart thought it'd be funny to slap the ICEE out my hand. Bunt and me bought the special Major League cups every week and stacked them on our windowsills. We were waiting for Hank Aaron, our favorite Atlanta Brave. Bunt looked at me that day and then down at the red ICEE on the blacktop parking lot. Then he looked at that big old boy and his face went cold and hard like stone. When Bunt took a step forward, the boy turned to leave, laughing over his shoulder like he wasn't scared.

He has that same look now when he sticks his finger in my chest. "You disappoint me, son," he says.

Now Debbie climbs on the block too and puts her arm around Bunt, "Hey you guys, let's go swimming."

"Crap," Stephen says. "You all are the wishyist washyist bunch I've ever seen... *Although,* I do like the idea of leaving them Whitehall pricks wandering around out here."

"How about the City Pool?" Bunt asks loudly, for everyone, but keeps his eyes on me.

Stephen says, "No way. Too many kids pee in there." He's right 'cause I've done it myself.

"Let's go in the river," says Debbie. We're not allowed to swim in the river, but we don't need parents to tell us that. Paul says no right away and his brother calls him a candyass and pushes him down again.

"My daddy let me go swimming at a boatlanding downriver," Debbie says. "It's really calm there."

"What you think?" Bunt asks, still staring at me. I don't want to look like a candyass so I say it's fine. Bunt asks everybody else and they all say okay and Debbie nods yes like her head is on fire.

We're leaving and I turn around at the head of the trail and see Debbie standing on my block. She's staring at a group of high school boys who float by on inner tubes. They scream and reach for one another and one of them hoowees and slaps the water when he sees her. I don't like that he does that and I kick a big pine root, more mad at being mad than anything else.

We ride our bikes through a long tunnel of blackberry bushes. The dirt road to the landing is under a roof of oak trees and moss and Bunt and me ride slowly behind the others in lazy Ss, in and out of circles of sunlight.

Bunt says, "Since Hank broke it, you'd think they have his cup in by now."

"I know," I say. "We ought to be checking every morning."

I'm thinking how many ICEEs we've had to drink and how many deposit bottles we've had to collect to buy them. And still no Hank Aaron. Not even after Hank broke the record.

It happened just last week. I'd been watching the game with my Daddy and his friend Earl. When The Hammer came to bat, Earl said, "I wish somebody would just shoot that boy." I thought he was talking about me, 'cause maybe I was blocking the TV where I sat on the floor. But that wasn't it at all, he wasn't even looking at me. Wasn't even looking at the TV. And then The Hammer nailed it, number 715, and I tell you what, I about came out my skin. I was jumping up and down and hollering like a fool when I noticed how quiet it was.

I went to the kitchen to call Bunt and I could hear them. My daddy told Earl he thought he'd never see the day. "Just ain't right," he'd said and there was a meanness to his voice. I saw once where John Wayne was after Indians that kidnapped his niece. Boy did he hate those Indians. I'd never heard a good guy sound so hateful and angry and that's what Daddy sounded like. I put the phone down and ran across the complex, along the way running into Bunt. Him already on his way to me.

I look at Bunt now as he leans way out over his handlebars, weaving back and forth.

"How long you think before somebody breaks 715," I ask.

10

"Shoot. Long time I guess," he says, steering slowly back and forth with his elbows. "Look how long the Babe held it. We'll probably be dead 'fore anybody breaks 715."

I've never been to the boatlanding before, so it's surprising how the flats of the river are so different. There's fewer trees so the sky is open and everything shimmers like the beach. The water plant's diversion dam is downriver and before it the water is wide and calm. Midriver is a tiny island covered with moss and rocks and two huge pine trees.

The others are already in the water as Bunt and me drop our bikes. The twins are on the putout, splashing each other like a couple of spastic lunatics. Debbie is floating on her back further out.

"How ya doin', Deputy?" I yell. Her ears are in the water so I don't think she hears me, but now I see her hand floating out beside her. She's giving me the finger.

Bunt goes screaming into the water and swims out to Debbie and squirts water on her face with his mouth. I wouldn't want him spitting on my face like that.

"What you waiting on, Case Man?" he yells. I'm always surprised to see Bunt swimming: Daddy says most colored people are scared of the water.

We have splash wars for a while and play Marco Polo and then take turns pairing up for Chicken. I like Chicken the best. I give Debbie a hard time, but I love the way she feels sitting on my shoulders.

After a while we see two turtles walking down the concrete putout. Just plain as you please, like it's their own private driveway. We take them up on the dirt road to have races when Bunt notices that Debbie's gone. We didn't see her get out of the water and her bike is still here. Everyone stands quiet, looking around, but there's nowhere to hide. A huge kingfisher flies down before us, just a couple feet away, and we hardly even notice it.

Bunt is starting to look scared and that worries me because Bunt is never scared. Then he smiles at me and nods towards the island.

"Come on out, Witch Mama," I yell. And there she is, her dumb old head sticking out from behind one of the trees, laughing at us.

Stephen laughs and cups his hands around his mouth and calls out that she's a "turd." As she swims back, Stephen splashes her and Paul wants to know about the island. She says it's just the trees and rocks but maybe she did see a snake swim by. Paul doesn't like that.

Stephen says she has some major balls swimming out there, and I say it's because of her boobs. "You can't sink with boobs like that," I say.

"That's right," Debbie says. "Maybe this year when you sit on Santa's lap, you should ask for a pair of your own." Everybody laughs, even me after a minute, and Stephen pulls at the nipple places on his tee shirt, making imaginary boobies and we all laugh very hard.

Just then Debbie says we should race to the island. Stephen thinks it's a great idea right away, but Paul wants to know more about the snakes.

So Bunt does what Bunt does and asks everybody and everybody finally agrees. "*Wait a minute*," I say, looking out the corner of my eye at Debbie. "What if the winner gets to pick somebody to swim back naked?"

"Holy crap," Stephen says. "And I thought I was the pervert."

Bunt likes the idea, though, and when Bunt likes something it's a done deal. What I like is that it's *my* plan. I also like knowing I'm the best swimmer. I can beat everybody except maybe Debbie, but I'm pretty sure about her too. And after I win, I know exactly who's going to swim naked.

We all line up in the water beside the putout and stand just where the river floor drops off. Mud swirls up from our feet and drifts out into the dark water and everybody smiles like they know something the others don't.

Bunt holds up his hand, "On your mark... get set... go!" Debbie and me are in clean and shallow and come out together already in stroke. I look behind and see Bunt is a few feet back. The twins are still on shore, Paul slapping at Stephen, who's yanked down his shorts.

I'm moving good 'cause I can feel the water pushing at my scalp. Debbie stays with me though, so I bury my face and stroke harder. When I check again she's still with me and Bunt's a little closer too and the twins are still fighting on the banks. I'm swimming as hard as I can. Now I don't even come out for air. Suddenly I feel something on my leg and I kick it away and stop to make sure it isn't a snake. When I turn, Bunt and Debbie are floating behind me.

Suddenly the water is much colder and in that weird way you know without seeing, I know it's gotten very deep. I look around to get my bearings and feel the thing on my ankle again. This time I see it's Bunt grabbing at me and now I can feel how strong the current is. He pulls at my leg and Debbie is looking off at the island that's coming and going at the same time.

Bunt yells that we have to swim. "Let's go! Let's go!" he yells.

The floodgate sirens begin to wail and on shore a red light on a long white pole flashes like the bubble on an ambulance. Now the water will rise and even though Mama says cussing is for the weak-minded I yell "shit shit shit" over and over again. I say god damn too but only in my head. It's like a dream. One of those dreams where you're trying to run from something but you can't go nowhere.

"Let's go, Case Man," Bunt yells.

Where did this come from? The water was so calm, like the pond behind our old house on Redwood Drive. It must be some kind of suction from the dam. Or maybe from where the water goes deep around the island.

13

Bunt keeps yelling and the twins are on shore jumping up and down and waving their arms. Now I see a dark path down the center of the river to the dam, the lines of the current moving against the calm water. If we get pulled to the dam when the water rises we're done for.

Debbie and Bunt hit a whirlpool and are yanked further behind. Now I see red mud and root tendrils floating up from below and I know I'm over the long pointed tip of the island. The current bends the roots out of reach, so I force my way underwater to catch one.

Bunt sees I've anchored myself so he grabs Debbie and slams against the water in a wild side-stroke. Before they get very far, though, the current pulls her loose and she screams. She has that look I figure people must get when they know they're dying.

It's not something I decide to do, but I let go the root and swim into the current. Debbie grunts when we hit and I pull her tight by the waist, kicking and pulling against the current. I tell God we're just kids and we don't know any better. I say it'll kill our parents right along with us and the world will be a lesser place for somebody so beautiful as Debbie to be taken away. I tell Debbie it'll be all right and I hold her tighter and push my back against the current. I think maybe if I hold her tight enough, God will see that I love her and maybe that'll mean something.

I tell God everything I think He wants to hear when I notice the wakes splashing at our sides and the current moving past us. I twist around and Bunt is holding the back of my shorts with one hand and a root with the other. I didn't feel him pull over me when I swam past to get to Debbie and I didn't even feel him put his hand inside the waistband of my shorts.

Bunt's a good foot taller, so he's been able to pull the root further out. He pulls us through the water and tells me to put my arms around his neck and for Debbie to do the same to me. Then he disappears underwater and grabs a root further up and then another and another until we can all stand.

14

When we can manage to move, we sit near one of the trees away from the rising water. Debbie cries and I put my arm around her. It bothers me that she gets up and sits in Bunt's lap and puts her head on his shoulder. It doesn't really bother me, though, maybe not as much as all the little times she smiles at him in that strange way. Shoot, if she wasn't doing it, I'd go over there and sit in his lap myself.

Bunt finally nudges me and points at the putout where the twins are yelling at a man in a camouflage boat. He slaps me on the back and says, "I guess I get to choose who goes back naked."

I start to laugh but he gets that look again. "Come on, Case Man, you better get them trunks off before the boat gets here."

Maybe the man is drunk, but he hardly seems to notice that I climb in the boat buck naked. I sit in the front with my back to everyone. Bunt and Debbie snicker and Debbie makes kissing sounds. I'm holding my folded shorts over my private parts and I want to laugh but I can't. I feel mad, strange mad. Not because they're laughing at me, and not because Bunt is actually making me go through with this. I'm just mad is all. Mad at everything. Bunt puts his hand on my shoulder and squeezes. "Got to give you credit, Case Man," he says. "Can't say I'd go through with this." Debbie agrees and rubs a soft circle on my back and I'm thinking how lucky we are. How lucky I am. And I'm thinking how stupid it is to be mad when you don't even know why.

§ § §

Mr. Jacobs is a freelance writer in Columbia, South Carolina. He has worked in the corporate world as a public relations and public information writer. His educational background is in creative writing, literature in English, and psychology. He is the recipient of an award for excellence from the South Carolina Press Association.

WARREN

by Joseph Young

I stutter. Okay? I juggle for a living and I wear suspenders and a tartan beret. Okay? I'm fat. My mouth tastes like ash from swallowing fire. And I can't keep my thoughts off Karin. She's my juggling partner, beautiful. She's Dutch and she's a lesbian. Okay? Is that okay?

This morning I'm in my room, sleeping. The floor begins to swim beneath the futon; the plaster cracks; the windows tear into murderous triangles. This is it, I think. I'm dead. Right now. 9.0 on the Richter.

I throw off the covers and bang through my door. I cross the hall and bang through Karin's. She's in bed with her girlfriend. They are sitting up, holding each other's hands, eyes on the trembling walls. Their four pink breasts shine in the white morning light.

The shaking stops and the city wails with car alarms. The girls, pillows to their chests, are staring at me. At my penis stiff in my underwear. "No!" I say. "It's the fear. I'm afraid." My ears burn with blood.

In the corner are three juggling axes. They have no blade, blunter than butter knives. I pick them up and start to juggle. Why? I don't know. I don't know.

The girls watch and they begin to laugh. I'm ridiculous. It's absurd. I'm in my underwear with a hard on. I'm terrified. Don't know what I'm doing. And they smile. They laugh. Oh god, that lovely bathing light, they laugh.

§ § §

Joseph lives in The City That Reads, just uphill from the greasy trickle of the Jones Falls. His work has appeared in previous issues of Literary Potpourri, Mississippi Review, Opium Magazine, and Small Spriral Notebook. He can be reached at youngjoseph21@hotmail.com.

FIRE

by David Toussaint

The deer aren't right on Fire Island. They're beautiful, yes; mythological wonders, and to gaze upon them from a distance is to witness the perfect form of God's capricious hand. But look a little closer and a different creature comes into view. Their eyes have lost the spark of forest life, and their once-shining gold coats seem burnt brown and toxic, as if the very air that sustains them has contaminated their skins. They are rampant here, always have been, but their stay is overplayed and unwelcome, leftovers from a time when there was space for them. If you dare get close enough to touch one, its eyes betray what's left of its composure, and you realize it has no place to flee.

San Francisco, 1981

Daniel, removing the contents of his locker on the last day of acting class, untaped the Brooke Shield's Calvin Klein ad from the metal door. He would take it with him as a reminder. The ad epitomized his ideas of New York. There, he mused, he'd find real theater, true actors, and glamorous people who would flock to his charm. He'd heard of mens' after-hour clubs and blue-lit private rooms. Someday, he thought, someday.

When he looked up, Bradley, the teacher's aide, appeared to his right, smiling, leaning against the arched door, arms folded casually over his chest.

Daniel had never seen a man more beautiful. In class, he often stared at Bradley's perfect body-- muscles puffed out in circles, flat stomach accented by khaki shorts that tented up unusually high when he sat, always on the floor, cross- legged with his knees up. When Bradley spoke in his low, instructive voice, it was as if he'd developed a hard-on just for you. He wore sandals every day, and his long, sculpted legs sprouted the same shiny blond hair that

19

covered his head. Each strand seemed bright and wet, like his eyes, reflecting little drops of light that gave the appearance of just having come from a long swim or a warm shower. Bradley was twenty-three, and for Daniel, he was the dream of youth's ache; someone a gawky, undeveloped seventeen-year-old could never possess.

The sound of laughing students running through hallways echoed outside the locker room, mixed with the scent of fresh linen, disinfectant and soap. Summer sun bloomed inside Daniel's head.

"Hi there," Bradley said.

"Hi." Daniel blushed and stared inside an empty locker.

"I wanted to thank you for taking our class. You were an excellent student."

"Oh. Thanks. I enjoyed it."

Bradley 's gaze swept over the ad in Daniel's hand. "Do you like him?"

"Who?"

"Calvin Klein." Bradley took the ad from Daniel, brushing an elbow against his arm. "I think he's sexy."

"I don't know. I've never seen him."

"You're kidding. He's on the island all the time."

"What?"

"Fire Island. Don't tell me you've never heard of it." Bradley tilted his head toward Daniel and lowered his voice. "You'd love it."

Daniel pictured a piece of deserted land with flames on every side. "Where's that?" said Daniel.

"New York. Long Island, actually. It's where all the men go."

20

"Really?" Daniel tilted his own head slightly. Bradley's lips were inches away.

"Really!" Bradley laughed and leaned back. "I spend my summers there. I'm leaving tomorrow."

"Tomorrow? Wow. That's so soon."

Bradley laughed harder and took in Daniel from top to bottom.

"You're so funny. Maybe I'll see you there sometime. 85 Beach End Walk."

"New York's a long way away. I hope so."

"Anyway, I have to go." He grabbed Daniel's arms and kissed him on the lips. "Good-bye, beautiful."

Beautiful.

"Bradley?" Daniel stopped him at the doorway. "When are you coming back?"

Bradley grabbed the top of the doorframe with both arms and leaned in. His tank top revealed strong triceps and underarm hair.

"Who says I'm coming back?"

When he disappeared, Daniel closed the locker and stared at his reflection in the metal door.

"Fire."

Fire Island, 1991

Daniel was fixated on his reflection in the mirror, and smiled. He knew others around him were, as well. He'd keep this smile for the entire weekend.

"Come along, virgin. It's time for Tea" Anthony called from

the gate at the Pines' outdoor gym. They both wanted to get a quick workout before nightfall, Daniel even more adamant about it than his friend. He'd only been here an afternoon, yet already admired on the beach and catcalled to as he walked along the wooden roads that connected each shrub-hidden house. Shirtless, in butch-looking Timberlands that were far too warm for June, Daniel felt like he'd arrived in a magic kingdom. Tanned men in draw-stringed bathing suits smiled at him from behind Ray-Ban sunglasses. Everything here was meant for pleasure-his pleasure-the sun on his back, the chlorine-scented pools against naked skin, the cube-clinking drinks, and the men with chiseled faces and heated eyes. They were the same men from high school, peeling their shorts off in the locker room, slapping ripe butts with towels and turning around to show off erections. The same men, but free, in a world that would defy gravity should it dare get in their way.

"Danny?" Anthony called again. He'd adopted this nickname for his friend as soon as they'd arrived. "We need to get there early so we can sit on the ledge. That way all the boys can see us."

"I'm coming," Daniel said, turning around to confirm that no fat hung over his shorts. "I just wish I had a better butt."

They walked along the road toward Anthony's house and greeted everyone who passed. Men carting groceries in red wagons, body-building couples in matching Speedos, the occasional solo guy in a tank top and cut-offs. "Heading for the Meat Rack," Anthony would whisper after they passed. Daniel only recognized a handful of people from his gym in Chelsea, and he was happy to let Anthony play host. Besides, Anthony was thirty-four, dark-haired and handsome, and had a full share with a pool. When anyone stopped and kissed him, they turned to Daniel next like he was the younger, just-blossoming sister, someone whom they had a full weekend to court and make their own. Daniel knew he'd been rewarded when Anthony invited him, he just hadn't realized how much of a prize he'd be.

"Anthony, what do you wear to Tea?" he said, as they

turned the corner onto Beach End Walk.

"No eyeglasses. If you trip over someone, all the better."

They stepped up to the gate in front of the share. Daniel spotted a deer.

"Anthony, look!" Daniel leaned over the fence and his friend grabbed him by the shorts.

"Don't get near it."

"What do you mean? It's beautiful. It's not even scared."

"God, you are new." Anthony shrugged his shoulders and walked toward the house. "You can't touch them. They have ticks."

Daniel followed, then turned around and looked at the deer. He walked back to the gate and leaned over the fence. The deer looked up and met Daniel's eyes. Daniel checked to make sure no one was watching, then leaned over and patted the deer on the forehead. The animal pulled back, and, startled, Daniel jumped. He ran toward the house and into the shower.

The sun spotlighted Daniel and Anthony. Their beach chairs were laid out on the sand, and Anthony brought along a martini shaker and two glasses, perfect for three o'clock cocktails. Neither of them had gotten up till noon, and after a quick cup of coffee, they set out to claim their territory. Anthony winced at Daniel's suggestion that they stay by the pool.

"Daniel, it's a perfect eighty-degree cloudless day. The boys will all be flocked near the water."

"So what time did you get home last night?" Daniel asked, applying a dab more Coppertone number four to his shoulders.

"Three. And you?"

"I don't remember, I was so drunk."

"Last I saw you, you were lip-locked with that kid from California. He looked all of seventeen."

"Do you blame me? He was so fucking cute."

"Did you have sex?"

Daniel looked at the water. Several men had jumped in and wrapped bathing suits around their necks.

"Yeah. It was great. On the beach."

"Oh God," Anthony laughed. "I knew you'd be a slut. And with a minor, no less. It's a good thing they don't have any rules out here."

They laughed even harder, knowing that fear would creep into silence. Momentary, slicing fear that could drown out the loudest beach radio. It sat between them, the uninvited guest, waiting introduction. Anthony addressed it first.

"Were you careful?"

"Oh...yes. Of course. Condoms all the way." Once he spoke, he couldn't brush the guest away.

"Do you ever worry about the other guys? You know, the ones who didn't know."

Anthony turned over on his stomach. His back was red.

"Things are better now. Why?"

"I was thinking about this guy. He was so beautiful. And he was here from the beginning. I don't know how anyone like that could be okay."

"Have you tried to contact him?"

"I don't even know his last name."

"Cheer up, Danny. Maybe he'll show up one day, walking along the beach. Healthy, happy, and madly in love with you."

"That's my dream. By the way, Anthony, those condoms I mentioned..."

"Yes?"

"Extra large."

They laughed again. Anthony poured two more drinks into oversize glasses and toasted their paradise. The uninvited guest flew off into the sea.

Daniel wasn't enjoying the party, but even at three a.m. he refused to leave. Tomorrow meant going home to New York, where there'd be rules and time frames and even secrets he'd have to keep. He ordered another rum punch from the shirtless bartender and walked out to the pool area overlooking the ocean. He stepped up to the railing and looked out at the moonlit ocean. The waves were crashing violently on the shore, and the drone of partyers behind him sounded disconnected from the night. As he took a few more sips, it became all one male voice, a hostile, cold voice that grew both louder and farther away at the same time. Daniel placed his drink on the railing and kept looking at the ocean. He realized he had no idea what lay beyond. Long Island jutted out from the city at a right angle, and he wasn't sure if he was looking toward Europe or South America. He wished he'd brought a map.

"Hey there." A man had walked up beside him and leaned against the railing. He was handsome, with dark hair, wearing tight shorts and no shirt. "You're awfully quiet. Aren't you having fun?"

"I'm just a little disoriented."

"Oh God, what did they put in your drink?"

"No. I was trying to figure out if we're looking east or south."

"In that case, maybe you should have another one."

"Seriously. Do you know?"

"I know that you're about the hottest guy at this party. God I'd love to take you somewhere and just nail you."

Daniel stared at the water.

"You there?"

Daniel turned toward him. "I'm sorry. I was thinking about someone."

"Uh-oh. Another broken heart on Fire Island. Should I leave?"

"No. It's not important."

"That's good. I'd hate to think you were cute *and* deep."

Daniel laughed. "Thanks. You're pretty hot too."

"My name's Tony, by the way."

"Daniel. Nice to meet you."

"Is this guy you're thinking about your lover? Not that I care; I just need to know if you'll want breakfast."

"No. Just a guy I used to know. I was wondering if he was around tonight." He took a sip and realized he'd picked up the wrong glass. "I'm sorry. I just took your drink."

Tony laughed. "That means you've already gotten a taste of me." He pressed his leg against Daniel's. "Have another sip."

Daniel obliged, then looked back at the ocean and saw him. He was walking alone at the edge of the water, barefoot and wearing only shorts. He held sandals in one hand and a blanket and a bottle of wine in the other, like he'd just gotten up from a day at the beach. Daniel leaned over to try and get a better look. In the moonlight he could see his still-perfect form. Even after all these years he felt acute longing, seeing Bradley. But his shyness returned and he felt all too sober. He drained his own glass, leaned over the railing, and called out hello.

The man stopped. He turned to look at Daniel, and smiled broadly. "Hey, Beautiful. Nice to see you again. Come down here and join me."

Daniel turned around to excuse himself, but Tony had vanished. He turned back around and Bradley was gone.

Daniel jumped over the railing. He looked around and saw no one. There were stairways lined up along the beach, each leading up to tiny roads that looked exactly the same.

"Bradley!" he called, then yelled with his hands cupped to the sides of his mouth. But only the slosh of the ocean answered him. Daniel tripped, running in the sand. The beach was deserted and the music got louder, so he picked himself up and headed back to the house. Tony's drink was still on the railing. He guzzled it and joined the party.

***

Danny packed his bag, hung-over from the night before, and headed for the six o'clock ferry. The housemates were still asleep, so he stepped out quietly, patting two poodles that whimpered on the deck chairs. They looked ill, the whites of their eyes lined by red, sticky liquid dripping from the lids.

He closed the gate behind him, walked down the path to the road, headed for the dock. It was muggy and overcast, and he was glad to be leaving. He felt like something was pulling him back, like he was moving through a film of humidity but not getting closer to the ferry. He wanted to run. There were tall green weeds on either sideof him that hid each house. No one talked about the shrubs, and Danny hadn't a clue as to what they were. They seemed indigenous to the island, hiding excess without the slightest bloom or color to disguise the ugliness behind them. A deer appeared out of the woods.

Danny stared at her, unable to avert his eyes. Somewhere

opera music wafted from a phonograph. It was five o'clock in the morning, and the only other sound was the thumping beat from the disco, which would continue till daylight. Down Harbor Walk, a drunk stumbled home, rejected no doubt, in a night that held off dawn like the enemy.

This was Daniel's last day on the island, the end of what seemed an endless summer of tanning on the beach, barbecues at his friend's share, and cocktails and boy-watching at High Tea. He'd been to Fire Island Pines only once before, and in the past several years had refused all invitations. He'd been told by friends that he thought himself superior to the party crowds who visited. But no one seemed to suspect his fear that just by stepping off the ferry and coming to this land, he'd become one of them-- and hadn't it been true?

The ferry seats were puddled with dirty rainwater. The older man next to Danny wore leather pants with a leather, sleeveless top, as well as a studded black belt and a dog collar around his neck. His muscular arms were blotched with green tattoos that matched the Formica tables, rooting him to the boat. He smelled like cum and grease. Danny tried to imagine what he did in the city, yet nothing came to mind. This man belonged to the island, probably always had, and Danny noticed that his gaze was firmly ahead, never wandering out the window to the other world.

The only other person to board was a slight woman of about fifty, with peroxide-blond hair, a creased face and a heavily tanned, freckled body. She wore cut-offs and a red bikini top, her small breasts sunken in like rotten fruit. Two German Shepherds leashed at her side fell asleep as soon as she sat down. She put on black sunglasses and turned to face the window.

Danny looked through his worn knapsack for something to read. He noticed a piece of paper crumpled at the bottom. He fished it out, unfolded it, and held up the old Brooke Shields Calvin Klein ad. He felt a visceral jab of pain and through the glossy paper, realized there was handwriting on the back. He turned the ad over, and read the words scribbled in black felt pen. "Bradley Daniels, 85 Beach End Walk. Fire Island. Hope to see you there."

He jumped from his seat, grabbed his knapsack and bag and ran to the front of the boat, jumped onto the dock and headed for the boardwalk. There was still no light, and the sound of the disco increased. He flew past white street signs-Ocean Walk, Bay Walk, Harbor Walk-the boardwalks identical on the surface, singularity identified only by the names printed on the signs, names for the graves piled within. He ran all the way to the edge of the Pines, where the woods took over, when he found it on the left.

Garbage cans and mailboxes were aligned on both sides and the slap of ocean waves grew louder. The salt air sprayed his face and the fog was as thick as thread. The disco beat turned into a steady thump in his heart. Signs for 81, 82, 83, and 84 moved by. 85 would be on his right. He approached the gate, stopped, and looked back. An antlered buck stared at him from the corner, then darted off. He pushed open the gate which led to several paths. It was impossible to know which one led to Bradley. He followed the sound of running water, bypassing a white wood house, searching beyond it.

The clearing was bordered by forest and shrouded in fog which shifted to reveal Bradley standing naked in the morning light under an outdoor shower, arms resting on his head. Bradley smiled as Danny walked into the clearing and stepped inside the circle of water, so close that their breathing interlocked. Bradley slowly undressed him. Danny was safe, naked and surrounded by fire. Bradley wrapped his arms around him as the water sheathed them from the heat. He touched Danny's lips.

"I knew you'd eventually find me," Bradley said. He took Danny's face in his hands and kissed him before he entered him.

"Fire."

Fire Island, 2001

Bradley woke up in a sweat. The covers were off and he realized he was still fully erect. It was five in the morning. Anthony was asleep next to him. He got up, put on a pair of boxers, and walked outside. It was dark out, but the sound of the disco thrummed through the night air.

"What are you doing up?" Anthony had followed him, and was standing next to the gate in his bathrobe. Bradley could already smell coffee being brewed.

"I'm sorry. I couldn't sleep. Go back to bed."

"Something wrong?"

"I was dreaming."

"What about?"

"Back in San Francisco, there was this guy. I remember telling him about this place. He was just a kid, but you could tell he'd be the type who'd end up here."

"So?"

"I dreamed he was on the island, and that he kept searching for me."

"I don't get it."

"It's my fault."

"What?"

"He's dead."

"What are you talking about?"

"About ten years ago, I was out really late at the disco. Drunk as hell. It was that weekend you and I almost broke up. I was so mad at you I ended up fucking around with someone."

"Bradley, we both..."

30

"It was him. I recognized him right away. I didn't even say anything. I just took him out to the beach and fucked him. Hard."

"You weren't safe?"

"He wouldn't even let me put a condom on. He was so seduced by the island, I could have done anything to him."

"So why is any of this your fault? You're not infected."

"Tony, he might have survived me, but there's no way he'd survive the rest of this place."

"That's still not your fault..."

"The next night, I was walking on the beach-I'd been out all day. I saw him up at one of the houses, at a party. I wanted to talk to him, to tell him to be careful."

"How come you didn't?"

"Because you were standing next to him. I was still mad at you, so I got pissed off and ran away."

"Bradley, come to bed."

"It's weird too because that part wasn't in the dream at all, and that's the only time I've seen him since."

"You probably blanked that whole weekend out of your head. Remember? I was fucking around with everyone too, and the next week I got the results of my test. God, who knows how many guys I nailed that weekend."

"Tony, I told him to come here. You should have seen the sparks in his eyes."

"Bradley, you have no idea what happened to this guy. He might be living happily ever after. Maybe someday you'll see him walking on the beach, healthy as anything."

"That's the dream."

"Come inside and have some coffee."

"In a minute."

Anthony kissed Bradley on the cheek and walked away. Bradley spotted a deer in front of him, staring directly into his eyes. Her coat looked golden brown and shiny, just washed from the night's rainfall. He thought about petting it, but knew Anthony would scream at him if he found out, like he did on his first trip to the island. He smiled as Anthony's Puccini floated from the bedroom. He heard a twig snap near him and saw a drunk stumbling home. Bradley was thankful that his partying days were over and that Anthony was still well; that morning was here and his head was clear. In a place that held off dawn like the enemy. He heard the coffee percolate and turned to look at the condominium he and Anthony had shared for twenty years on 85 Beach End Walk. The sun peered through the trees and the thump of the disco died. Bradley almost turned back to look at the deer, but knew instinctively that it was gone.

§ § §

David Toussaint is a freelance writer, director, actor, and producer living in New York City. His fiction has appeared in the e-zines "Outsider Ink," "The Prose Menagerie," as well as the literary journal "Snow Monkey."

Three years ago, he wrote and directed a one-act play, "Backstage Bitches," which ran for two consecutive summers in Manhattan. He's a contributing editor and travel writer for Conde Nast Publications, and is currently at work on a new play. He'd like to thank Beverly Jackson for her patience, faith, and endless "fire."

YIELDING FRUIT (for Nealey)

by P. Gomes

She is plum.
Electric:
ions, atoms,
neutrons and neurons
buzzing - zzzzzt!
shoot from her thunderous cropped hair
when she enters a room.
Smiles a strong-toothed grin and the voltage
kicks up another few kilowatts.
Bounce, bouncy, bouncier
on unseen springs, she rallies
with a firm handshake and a pamphlet.
There's a Cause, always a Cause
and "of course, it's important!"
she admonishes behind bifocals
secured by a hemp cord.
Ever the rebel, the hippie, the feminist.
Seeds left fallow by a life choice
and the appeal of softer hands,
she mothers her familiars instead,
birthdays always remembered,
anniversaries calendarized,
we are gifted
with purple ribbons.

She is plum -

lilac, lavender, mauve, violet, amethyst...
wine. Aged to perfection.
She is
Mother's secret kept
from the Garden Club, a cross to bear
but good for lifting heavy things
and changing the diapers of now great-nieces
and nephews.

She is folk songs
and the spoken word that echoes
off art-hung walls framed
by convict hands
in old buildings with blackened windows,
one political visit away from condemnation.
Applause, applause, applause.
Existing for the annual two-week vacation
on the Cape
where she'll bathe
in rainbows,
sidewalk sketches,
and freedom.

She is
plum.
The first bold crocus
(purple, of course)
pushing boldly through Winter's white quilt.
In dusk,
she's come to terms
with life

and closet doors.

TOURISM TAKES A HOLIDAY
by P. Gomes

©2003 CapeAnnPics.com

It's snowing,
but it ain't the good snow
of Christmas card fame and snowball fights. Angels and forts.
Hot chocolate with a dollop of whipped cream under a chenille throw.

It's the snow-changing-to-freezing-rain-by noon snow
It stings, burns if you're out in it long enough.

Battleship gray, the sky that matches the ocean
and the harbor is full.
Scallopers, trawlers moored,
anchored against the onslaught of liquid shrapnel.
Battleship gray, the faces forced to stay
and take this time
to mend the nets
toss back a few pops
and compare wind-laden skies seen before. "Storm?" This ain't a storm;
Lars, you call this a storm?"
Lars shakes his head, comprehending the American banter through
Swedish ears
while sipping dry Portuguese wine.

Fat gulls fight with pigeons over gurry scraps,
white feathers ghostly against the steel backdrop.
Squawk in competition with the Babel-voiced fishermen.

Whores adorn the rough-hewn planks of the wharf.
No "Miss Kitty" these. Homegrown coasties acclimated in yellow-slickers
and Timberlands.
Find a calloused hand needing the warmth of softer flesh and offering
a long dollar in return. Kiss the cracked lips of the sea; taste the dash of
salt from Neptune's table.
Grab some quick cash if they can before the sidewalks ice up. Mascara
streaks in the wet.

It's snowing. But it ain't the good snow.

§ § §

35

A writer of dark fiction, P. Gomes has recently appeared in Golden Wings 2002 - An Anthology of World Poetry. Ms. Gomes currently resides on the coast of Massachusetts, an area rife in history and folklore where she is working on the first in a series of three horror novels.

She can be reached at: pag73@hotmail.com.

DR. DICK SOMEBODY

by Marc Phillips

He tells the thing to Steve, an anesthesiologist, as they're changing clothes in the locker room. He's unsure why he's telling a colleague at all, but especially an anesthesiologist. The locker room; it's called that for a reason--all the lockers--but it's asinine nonetheless. Actors have greenrooms. Wouldn't you think doctors would warrant more than a goddamn high school label for their private area? Doctors grab coffee, steal minutes to eat bagels and bullshit with other doctors; tell anesthesiologists things they should not--in locker rooms.

"I told them, Steve, the whole spiel. I tied it in with the risk probabilities, the outside chances, the five percent language on the 'permission to treat' form they signed. I said, 'Mr. and Mrs. Whatever,' I said, 'I know that losing a child is hard--the hardest thing in the world--but I think you made the right decision.' I told them to call me if they needed to talk. Shit, I hope they don't call."

"Home number? Or your service?" Steve asks.

"Here at the hospital. Anyway, I *don't* know, see? I have no clue what it feels like to have a kid with congenital heart defects. I wouldn't be able to guess. When it croaks, does the father feel like his innards are shredded without anesthesia--or is it numbness like OD'ing on morphine? Or worse, or not as bad, or different altogether?"

Dick is still holding his right shoe. Completely dressed, and here he sits for--how long? five, ten minutes--talking to Steve the mother-loving anesthesiologist about *real* doctor stuff with an untied Nike in his hand, strings dangling. Steve stares at him, mouth slightly open, shirt half-buttoned. An older doctor, a seasoned surgeon, would not be noticing Steve.

"You're being too hard on yourself, Dick. Go home and sleep it off. You lost one. You'll save another." Steve closes his locker and leaves without finishing off the buttons.

Dick puts the shoe on, ties it, and walks outside to his bicycle. Did he close his locker? Fuck his locker. What's in it? Scrubs. Candy bars. He weaves between parking dummies on his way to the road. He hopes he has closed his locker and locked it. Somebody will steal his candy.

At the top of the hill, in front of Trinity Episcopal Church, he changes gears. Dick is in that gear that makes him feel he's contributing to the Earth's rotation with every lusty, satisfying downward heave. His big thighs, hard with years of this since his residency days, don't register the intensity of it, but soon he's passing cars.

His bike has purpose, beyond the benefit to his physique. This is the unequivocal zone, the part of his day that musters all prior parts into a line by descending order of importance; or makes all things irrelevant which are not now indicative of absolutes like stop or go; diesel fumes or brake dust; pedaling life or stale morgue death. Is he about to weep? Oh, Christ on the cross, he hopes not. He remembers his third year of medical school better than he recalls breakfast this morning.

Dr. Allen Rothschild saying, "You will not know, until the first one dies. Nobody knows if he can take that. If you're lucky, it will happen early."

It hadn't though, had it? He'd seen trauma vics bite it, but half their chest and most of their blood was on the street somewhere. They were dead before anyone called the ambulance. He'd seen seventy and eighty-year-olds with worn-out tickers and Pall Mall lungs give it up on a heart monitor, their children and grandchildren watching, blubbering. In such cases, a physician was requisite only to officiate the passing, so to speak. Dick had assisted surgeons he privately blamed for killing people. Yet, he had made it this far without ever having to seriously examine his own skill as a healer, a human mechanic, absent the shortcomings of technology, and the mistakes of other men. When people teetered precariously between being and ending, did he throw them a line, or did he throw them a twenty-five thousand dollar bloody send-off? But that smooth skinned little boy with the blue, trusting eyes? Christ! He can't even remember his name.

Dr. Rothschild asks, "What use has a surgeon for names? They can be charts, successes, and failures. Or, they can be friends; in which case, quit and go home."

Dick's home. They had bought it, Dick and Margaret (Maggie at Junior League functions) four years ago. A two story Georgian townhouse, and on the night of the closing they had sat on the carpet getting drunk in the elitist, regal emptiness of it. Margaret, drinking champagne from the bottle, had lamented that the only thing was, you know, some people did not consider a townhouse a real house.

"An honest-to-God house," she'd said. The night of the closing she'd said this.

Dick had asked her, "Is that right? And these people who would not consider my townhouse a house, they are who? Waste management engineers with lawns and lawn mowers to push around? They are trash men, Maggie, fucking trash men, and furniture salesmen, and cheesy insurance peddlers who can't afford a place in town. An honest-to-God half a million dollars."

Then he filled his mouth with Guinness and spit it in her face, and on the white turtleneck tube-top covering her breasts. She had recoiled initially, but then she just sat there wiping and blinking it out of her eyes, her nose all scrunched up. It was drying already when she had started crying. Her little shoulders jumped slightly and shuddered. Sour beer spittle was barely distinguishable from the scattered pretty freckles there, except in a measure of dignity, womanhood, taken before and after. The tears made tracks outlined in muddy brown down her cheeks and neck.

He helped her clean it off with toilet paper, the only thing in the place, and they fucked on the carpet--the first time in the new house. Or townhouse, she insisted on calling it

39

from thence, always the careful qualification. But there had been no way to get it out of her hair. She smelled of stout, forty-weight beer, as they humped. She hated beer, and considered herself above it. Dick caught whiffs of it now and then as they panted and fingered and pinched each other, and he had laughed.

She is asleep now, upstairs. Margaret, the sweet-tasting, simple woman he married, will not be Maggie until preened, bejeweled, and self-bestowed with all the ostentation his career afforded her. Dick puts his bike on his shoulder and walks with it across the hardwood floor littered with ancient Persian patterns to the washroom in back where he hangs it on the wall. He kicks his Nikes off in there as well. He takes off his Auburn sweatshirt and tosses it in the direction of the clothes hamper, or where he would have put the thing had anybody asked him.

He is naked from the waist up, his bottom half clothed in tight khakis and socks. He pauses at the hall mirror. He is chiseled, and graceful, and six feet tall. Not the classic picture of a 32-year-old cardio-thoracic surgeon at all; but the picture of this one, and no other. Dick is something to look at, but he has lately grown bored of looking at himself.

He stands at the fridge now. The door is open and there is Coke. No. Juice. No. Beer. No. Water in a pitcher with a filter on top. Maybe. Yes. He goes to the cabinet for a glass, and there is a cat between his legs. Its name is Jim, or Boots, or Spot, or didn't matter because cats will not come when you call their names. But he has a thought. He pours his first glass of water and drinks it immediately. He pours his second and carries it into the living room. He sits in the leather chair adjacent the couch, his reading chair. He places his glass on the table and turns on the lamp. The cat is beside the chair now.

He thinks of Mr. and Mrs. Whatever. What was their name? Their son was a Timmy? no Tommy Whatever. Dick briefly wonders did the closing surgical assistant sew the boy's chest with skill, or did she use big Frankenstein sutures? Her in a hurry to get home, or get a nap; and this being dead little Tommy Whatever.

Dick places his hand atop the cat's back. The animal thinks it's being petted. It inflates its chest. Dick waits. It exhales and he places his finger on one side of the rib cage, his thumb on the other. He does not squeeze, so the cat is not alarmed. He holds his finger and thumb steady and waits again. Inhale, shallower this time, exhale, and Dick closes the distance between thumb and finger. The cat gets spooked and tries to dart. Inhale, exhale, thumb and finger close enough now so the animal cannot draw the breath to screech. It digs little razor claws into the carpet, down to the jute backing. Some of them snag there and break off. Its head flails side to side, trying desperately to lay teeth into the vice at its ribs, because this is what animals do. The cat does not plead. It cannot. It boils over with rage and frustration. It thrashes. It shivers. It pees and shits a perfect little ball simultaneously. Then Dick can no longer feel its heartbeat. It is silent and still forever with big eyes and a gaping mouth. Dick leaves it beside his chair. He cannot tolerate the smell of cat urine.

On his way up the stairs, Dick thinks about the death of the animal. Does he feel like he wants to lash out, like Mrs. Whatever? No, not especially. He opens the hall door to the master bath. Does he feel the solemnity of soul, the profound devastation behind Mr. Whatever's single, long, insufferable tear? Nuh-uh. He smears Crest on his toothbrush, and he thinks he already knows why.

A. It's a cat.
B. He hates cats.

So, he feels what? He feels like pummeling the nasty little bastard with... With the Oxford English Dictionary, unabridged. Just thud down on its corpse over and over because it evacuated its bladder and bowels on the carpet. He spits in the sink and rinses his brush.

Dick takes off his socks and drops his pants on the bathroom floor. He drops his briefs. The door into their bedroom, opposite the side he entered the master bath, is still closed. There is a full-length mirror on this side of it. He looks at his cock. He isn't bored with that yet. It is pretty tonight; it hangs well. It moves a little as he thinks to it. The head undulates. Normally the bicycle seat and the tight briefs cause it to retract, to wrinkle. Tonight, it's almost like it's been hard. Recently. Dick smiles. He holds his genitals in one hand and closes his eyes. The nerve cluster near the head of his penis comes alive with a tingle. He sighs and opens the door.

Margaret is lumped beneath the down comforter, on her side of the bed. Dick eases under on his side and slides over to spoon behind his wife. She has on a thong and her bare cheeks are supple stimulation on his pelvis. His erection nuzzles its way between her legs. He drapes his big right arm over her slender frame, across her chest, beneath her breasts. He thinks, do I care for her? She moans in her sleep and pushes her ass into him.

Does he love her, like a parent would love a child? He thinks more of her than he does a cat, surely. But does he love her? She inhales with sleepy slowness, and exhales. Dick positions the vice jaw, made this time of his forearm and chest, perfectly around her rib cage and locks it at an unobtrusive width. Margaret inhales a tad shallower and, still asleep, exhales. He closes in a little more and holds like tempered steel. She is not much stronger than the cat, in that neither of them registers on his strength scale. Something triggers concern in the sleeping woman. She wiggles a little and cannot turn over. She exhales and he reduces the allowance of life a full inch this time. She moans in her sleep and he moans in her ear. He tightens the vice. Her lung capacity is cut to one tenth its norm. She starts to writhe. Her upper thighs grip his hard penis and twist, and ride. It feels nice.

Margaret's diaphragm spasms and a choked cough awakens her. She is conscious of two things at once, not knowing which to attend to first. There is a penis pressing on her labia majora, reaching for her clitoris. There is an arm clamped at her sternum, collapsing her lungs. She draws her left arm from under her body and slaps at the forearm restraining her.

She manages a choppy, "Di-ick?"

Dick releases her. She yawns, a reflex action of the

diaphragm.

She says, "That's too tight, baby. I couldn't breath." She reaches down and rubs his penis. "Mmm. I like that."

After sex, she says, "Wow. What a nice surprise. What's got you so randy tonight?"

"I don't know, Hon." He's behind her again, his right hand still wandering about her body, his left hand tangled in her hair.

"You have a good day at the hospital?"

"Not any better than usual." His hand slides from her hip and traces a faded suture line toward her pubic hair. He bites her earlobe. She stops his hand at the base of the scar.

"Mmm. You better stop that before you bite off more than you can chew, cowboy. Lemme up." She pats his thigh. He takes his arm off her.

She gets up and starts toward the bathroom, yawning again. He rolls over to his side of the bed and finds his sleeping spot.

Dick hears Margaret douching in the bathroom. He says to the closed door, "Maybe it's time we talk about trying again." He waits, nothing. "You hear me?"

The toilet roils. She sticks her head out the door.

"Dick, baby. We don't have to do that now, huh? Let's talk about it this weekend. At brunch, I promise. She winks at him and she closes the door.

He hears the shower come on.

"Hey! Hey, hang on!"

The shower goes off. Margaret opens the door with a towel wrapped around her and sighs. She looks at him, eyebrows raised.

43

"Hon, I think your cat shit beside my chair. You might want to go check on it before you take your shower."

She walks down the stairs wearing the towel and Dick buries his face in the unbleached Egyptian cotton pillowcase and holds back a sob with his whole mind.

This is death fucking with you, he thinks. It is what it is. You can handle it. You will not let this be a problem.

§ § §

Marc Phillips is a 30-year-old displaced Texas writer.

He holds most dear the belief that the majority of our best literature is yet to be written, and some of it was sung by the hair bands of the 1980's.

Marc can be contacted at: rms2@att.net.

This is his first published fiction.

HOW TO PUT A CAT TO SLEEP

by Michael A. Arnzen

First, you never actually use the words "sleep" or "death."
You circumvent them. You avoid eye contact and point at
charts and x-rays. You try to sell a little bit of hope, but
you let the illuminated plastic film contradict your words.
The lungs are half full of tumorous growth. The couple
standing there can see the balloon inside her airway, just
waiting to burst. You tap it with a pen to point out the
obvious, but the action speaks louder than your words. But
even more than this gesture, they can hear their pets
clotted pants and they can still feel the moist blood she'd
coughed up, slick between their fingers from all the
petting they're doing.

Next, you let them ask. Is it time? Should we do it? Please
give it to us straight: what are her chances?

Some things you have to figure out as you go along. That's
the part you hate most.

So you spill the beans in numbers and percentages. You
give them your trusty anecdote about a dog named
Buttercup who lived years after a similar diagnosis; you
then mention Petunia, who surprised you by croaking in
your arms when you put the thermometer up her bum. You
let them ask questions, but you mostly let them come up
with their own answers.

You leave them in the emergency room to talk to their cat
while you and your assistant go into the hidden recesses
of the clinic. Your assistants uncomfortably wipe old test
tubes and organize charts. You risk eye contact and that
says it all: they're gonna do it. You fetch the poison and
prep the anesthesia. Your main assistant grabs the tissue
box and rubber gloves.

When you return, the tears say it all. You ask what they
want to do anyway, because it isn't really you that's killing
the cat, it's them, and you want them to know that. The
husband assents and the wife just nods and loses

45

whatever she was holding back, pouring it into the cat with a hug. You explain the procedure and ask if there are any questions. There aren't any that you can answer.

You slide the blue needle in. To numb. Then the red one. To nod her off.

The cat blinks at the couple one last time. Slowly.

Eyes freeze half-open. The couple frowns in an unfathomable way.

You just nod and clench your teeth and balance your objective features against your empathetic eyes. When you withdraw the needle, blood leaks out in a way that only a dead body leaks it. You cover this up with cotton, but they see it.

Finally, you express your sympathies by reciting a Hallmark and then let the assistants explain the disposal and billing options.

As you return to your desk you realize that you've still got the red needle in your grip. There's still a little liquid unplunged, like hope. Not enough to save.

§ § §

Michael A. Arnzen has appeared recently in Vestal Review, Minima, 42opus, and Insolent Rudder. His poetry book, "Freakcidents: A Surrealist Sideshow,"is forthcoming from DarkVesper Publishing. Arnzen teaches writing and popular fiction at Seton Hill University. He was awarded the Bram Stoker Award for his first horror novel, "Grave Markings," in 1995. Visitors are welcome at his home page:www.gorelets.com. He can be reached at arnzen@gorelets.com.

NIGHTSPACE

by Susan Plett

the moon calls me
into this silken California dark
sings to me to embrace the stars
walk softly
lightly on the soles of my feet
in the gentle quiet beneath the trees

we are too large in lighted places
we interact with rooms full of furniture
that crowd out thought, voice

our deepest truths are nocturnal
bats curled in upon themselves
I enter the darkness without flinching
eager for the sandpaper rasp of truth
on the soft underbelly of fear

the bat unfurls his widespread wings
I take careful note of the shape of his ears
count the teeth in the warm pink mouth
test the sharpness of each small toenail
carry the weight and shape of him
into the cool gray dawn

§ § §

*Susan Plett refers to herself as an accidental poet - she
never aspired to write poetry, but her fiction got shorter
and shorter, and more image filled, and so she finally*

surrendered. Her work has appeared in *FreeFall, Canadian Writers Journal, StoryTeller,* and online at *Utmost Christian Writers.*

You can reach her at *brekke@elegantlogic.com* .

SUMMER RUSH
by Patty Mooney

49

Photo of Patty Mooney - by William Morton © 2003:all
rights reserved

Patty Mooney is a video producer, poet and artist living in
San Diego. Her works have appeared in Eclectica, Pierian
Springs, Branches Quarterly, LA Times, Post Magazine and
others. She was recently the featured poet at
www.writersmonthly.us. Contact her at
patty@newuniquevideos.com

DEEP SEA DIVING ON SUPER 8

by Martin Rutley

It took twenty minutes to get the guy from his house to the studio. Denny caught the whole trip on high 8, so I'm thinking I might cut some of that in with the final edit--give the piece that rounded feel I missed with 'Dandelion Trails'--maybe a few bars of MC5's 'Motor City is Burning' running over the top of it. I've taken free rein on this one, two hours in which I can do what the hell I like without answering to anyone. I don't mind keeping the boys informed, but they aren't going to bloody well call my shots. They get finished product just like the newspapers.

I left his children locked in with the wife. The kids don't seem too bad, but that wife of his is a real handful--bitch bit me on the fucking hand moving her back into the bedroom. She's going crazy, telling me I can take whatever I want, all the time figuring I'm the kind of guy can be bargained with. That's how it is with these kinds of people--no one's ever had the balls to let them know when they're screwed.

As a rule, we take nothing from the house. Occasionally, we'll find something that takes our eye, something we can drop into a few shots--a photograph, a piece of jewelry, a handwritten letter, something personal like that. Tonight, I'd taken a framed photograph of what must be his father vacationing in the South of France, short-sleeved shirt tucked into maroon colored slacks, broken blood vessels beneath his left eye.

Before we left the house, Frank knocked him about a little, nothing too heavy, a couple of slaps here and there--I've found it pays to show our hand from the word go. Once you've got your duct tape in place, you're ready move him from the house into the car, which isn't always 1-2-3 when you've got his family crawling the ceiling in an upstairs bedroom. Still, we managed it easily enough, and once you've got your man in the trunk of the car, you're on the home straight.

* * *

.

"You're #709 on their list, Mr. Rayner."

"What list? Whose?"

"I mean it's not my list; we just oblige them with the films. You're in excellent company --Rod Stewart, Liza Minnelli, Winston Churchill, Marilyn Monroe--they've an eye for originality, Mr. Rayner, for those with something new to say."

"I've nothing new to say, I assure you."

"You're far too modest, Mr. Rayner. Only last year, I was watching one of your shows in which you reunited a prostitute Mother with her runaway daughter, it was one of the most moving moments I've ever seen on a television screen."

"Thank you, but the daughter was dead within three months--shot a lethal dose of methylphenidate mixed with heroin, a 'speedball' I think they call it. "

"You've taken their eye, Mr. Rayner, and that's all there is to it."

"Whose? What do they want with me?"

"Well, let me ask you this, Mr. Rayner--have you ever seen the face of a newborn baby staring back at you from inside the helmet of a deep sea diving suit?"

"I haven't. Could I just go home now?"

"You haven't?"

"Of course, you're speaking purely in metaphorical terms--"

"Shit. Stop, stop" I move towards him, stepping into the shot. "Are you fucking ignorant? I told you not to look into the camera. You looked directly into the fucking camera."

That's the thing with guys like this--they've no idea what it means to work according to a few guidelines. Number one talk show host in the country and he's talking into the goddamned camera. I want him home by six a.m. and that's not likely to happen if I'm waiting around for him to pull his act together.

"I'm sorry, I can do it again," he says, shifting in his seat. "I'm a little nervous, that's all."

"Quit worrying about your fucking family," I tell him, getting right up close into his face. "Just say the lines as they've been given to you without looking into the fucking camera. Can you do that for me?"

It takes a good half hour to get the shots we need. The guy's all over the place, can't sit still in his chair, wants to know what's happening at home all the time. We keep the camera rolling, laying down some of the best 'don't-hurt-my-family' type drivel we've had in a long while.

The next scene is the pivotal point of the entire piece--I don't get this right and I've got the schmuck out of bed for nothing. Denny's switched to Super 8, mounting the camera in a stationary position, which we'll run at eighteen frames per second. We're looking for a static headshot of around two minutes, more if the guy can hack it.

He's shaking all over as we get him into the diving suit. Frank slips the helmet over his head, locking it into position with the lower half of the suit.

"Ok, move him over this way," I tell Frank. "Yeah, just about there. How's that look, Denny?"

"Yeah, I got him, don't let him move from there."

"Ok, I'm ready with the pump."

We'll have to move fast here, even with Frank supporting the lower half of his body, he won't last long standing in the suit.

"Ok, we're rolling."

I flick the switch, starting the pump that'll gradually fill the helmet with water through it's modified air inlet. I'm watching the monitor feed from the Super 8--a direct line from the image I've held in my head for more than three months. All we see now is the eyes, the rest hidden behind the static shell of the baby's smiling face.

Within the first minute, the water has traveled a good halfway up the inside of the helmet. Off camera, I watch Frank struggling to hold the guy still, both arms locked tight around his abdomen. He's throwing his arms about, beating the sides of the helmet with his fists-- reaching down to grab at Frank, at anything he can get his hands on.

I'm glued to the image on the monitor screen, getting big kicks from the way his eyes are shifting violently in their pre-fabricated sockets. I figure he's been without air for around forty seconds, not long enough to drown a man, but enough to have him thinking his number's up.

"A minute thirty, Ray."

"He's looking good, Denny. I need enough to run ol' blue eyes' 'Paper Moon' over this one."

Around two minutes ten, I give Frank the signal to get him out of the helmet. The guy falls to the floor the moment Frank gets him out.

"We've got a problem here," Frank yells, slipping the mask from off the guy's face.

"You're gonna tell me he's dead next, Frank?"

"He's dead, Ray." .

* * *

When the unexpected happens you've got to be ready to improvise, to make a decision and move on it without looking back. You give a guy too much credit and he'll slap you right back in the face, he'll turn his life in just so he can point out your mistake--piece of shit did everything he could to prove he was forty pounds too heavy and pushing fifty, his wife and kids never came into it.

I get Denny over with the super 8, he shoots several slowly revolving shots of our dead talk-show host, ending with a static sixty-second close up of the guy's face--I had to re-open the eyes myself, who the hell drowns with their eyes closed?

Within twenty minutes, we're heading back to the house, our man back in familiar territory, locked in the trunk. As Frank guides the car through the suburbs, I'm running the final scene over in my head. No more of these shorts, these half-assed teases. I tell Frank to save enough film for the upstairs visit--the big ending the boys down at the precinct have been waiting for. As I settle back into my reveries, Denny points the super 8 out through the windshield, its mechanical eye immortalizing all we allow it to see--given free rein, the responsibilities are frightening.

§ § §

Martin Rutley has been writing both poetry and short fiction for several years, largely influenced by writers such as William Burroughs and Greg Hollingshead.

He has been published in several magazines, including The Pedestal Magazine, Born Magazine and Soma Literary Review.

He can be reached at bluelightout2003@yahoo.co.uk.

MAYBE PLAY AROUND WITH THAT A LITTLE
by Jim Amos

She lets her mind wander into the 30-minute daily puzzle about pouring her thigh over his belly towards Jerusalem with painted lips pursed and eyes aglow, whispering slow wet frothy bubbling promises into his well groomed ears as a flock of Herons fly in from the south of nowhere to feed upon her inhibitions.

He slides along personality pathways like rum in a cocktail, slithering under the hemline of her battered self image to tease apart petals of an unrehearsed caught-on-camera saucy pantomime routine. *O no you shouldn't* the audience yells but she is pleasantly scorched, no going back as he infiltrates the headquarters and the hindquarters and the space between with quick flicks of a seventy-percent-accurate smart missile with deadly precision (and easily remedied imprecision) making her forget all the frequently asked questions of the day the month the year, forcing her to vote YES on all his pressed demands.

She shakes off her shoes her clothes her skin, she rips sinew and muscle and digs great holes in her bones revealing dramatic valleys of flesh. She proffers up her heart; he kicks her full of strawberries-and-cream-morphine with an easy-to-swallow satyr's stare; she doesn't know if he takes a bite - the lights are too grim and the stage so neatly decked in decadent props and the stench of lemonade and Indian summer.

Something like a warm hand comes swooping down from the sky to land on her curved spine leaning into the sun. She turns around, now waking, it is 'him', her boss, Mr. "*please call me Hank.*" She swoons, spins around, dances a dizzy waltz for a few years, blushes hard and tries to look austere thinking that will do the trick. A funny thing happens then because he winks and says O.K that he under*stands* and as he slinks away he feeds her the kind of smile that makes her feel like she is the cream of every soup, and the sky gives a satisfied burp as if to say *maybe play around with that a little.*

61

§ § §

Jim Amos is the kind of writer who will sit at the screen for so long that he only realises time has passed when he hears the inimitable echo of his own neglected stomach.

He also writes poetry and has been published at Snow Monkey, Pierian Springs, Clean Sheets, Tryst and Ultimate Hallucination. He can be reached at j_p_amos@yahoo.com.

CONVERSATIONS WITH YOUR PORTRAIT
by Ruth Mountaingrove

I cannot bring back that dream
or your photographed face
or that ambient time
when the matrix was love
when the fuel of sexuality
fired stone into alchemy
the passions of the moment
caught on this thin film.

I can wish to repeat
but cannot
for the interstices have changed
and we are both older
and younger.

So your photograph is now the dream
and what mistakes we have made
in focus, in timing,
in our openness or closing
are as permanent as this piece of paper.

I cannot bring back that moment
I am not a time traveler
going back to the Pleistocene
or forward into oblivion.

I am here at this interface
of our separate lives.
And when I reach toward you
to recreate this ambiance

I am stopped by the wall of time,
the rock hard years,
the frozen moment will not thaw.
And I am trapped in amber memory.

So we begin again
as strangers
I the photographer
you the photograph
as though we had just met
as though we do not know
as though we have no memory
no record from the past

And is this possible?
Yes. Yes. Because now
we are strangers.
I do not know you
or you me.
Rocks and walls
stand between us
and what I know is hearsay,
is gossip, is what I see.

We are new to this moment
this moment I hold in the camera,
my eye to the photograph,
My eye to your eye.

§ § §

Ruth Mountaingrove, a gifted performance poet, was Queen of the Humboldt county Poetry Jam and Slam in 1996, after which she retired so that the honor could go to someone else.

She is the author of two poetry books: Rhythms of Spring and For Those Who Cannot Sleep. Her work appeared in two issues of the Manzanita Quarterly. Ruth has a weekly radio show on KHSU which features women - locally, nationally and internationally.

AFLOAT

by KR Mullin

Leaving Alabama

In August, the woman's husband announced that they were moving. He'd been selling wallpaper throughout western Alabama and Mississippi, but a better territory had opened in Minnesota, and he'd gotten it and put their house on the market. The woman was further surprised by the fact that he'd made an offer on a rural property with a large, old house by a lake and that his offer had been accepted.

Although she'd lived in Birmingham all her 42 years, she tried to be pleased and only offered an argument against the expense, which would strain their already over-extended financial situation. She also pointed out that they could do with a smaller house now that their daughter was married and living in Florida and their son had moved to Kansas after graduating from college.

The woman's husband could not be bothered with such trivialities, so she went through the house and listed things she should do to increase its value:

Replace cracked window in back door
Empty attic and clean it
Paint bathroom
Attach new drawer handles in kitchen
Improve front yard
Refinish upstairs hallway floor

On Labor Day weekend, even though there had been no offers on their house, the woman's husband loaded the car with his necessities and left for Minnesota to start a new life while she stayed behind to tidy up the old one--packing some of it and disposing of the rest.

It took another month including two price drops before someone made an offer on their house. Even though it was lower than their asking price, the woman accepted, much to the dismay of her husband, and called the moving company. A week later, she told the real estate agent that the house was empty, and he stopped by for the key. He then offered her a ride to the bus station, and, when he learned that her bus didn't leave until 8:30, made some other offers which she declined.

Listings

The woman kept a small, spiral bound notebook in her shoulder bag for making lists, and the bus trip gave her plenty of time for considering some of her old lists as well as devising some new ones.

First, she started a page entitled "All the Stops from Birmingham to Duluth". This was a numbered list and began with "1. Birmingham". She also started another numbered list entitled "Places I've Lived" even though she thought she might have already listed these in a previous notebook.

Other lists were not numbered because there was no special order to the items. For instance, "Things to Do on a Farm near Duluth". This list began with "Read all of Oprah's books".

Because she'd planned her trip to include a visit with her son in Kansas, another page was entitled "Topics to Discuss in Kansas City" and began with "Thanksgiving? Christmas?"

Three-syllable Stops from Birmingham to Duluth

1. *Birmingham*
3. *Carbon Hill*
6. *Hamilton*
8. *Tupelo*

The woman's son had become a disc jockey at a small radio station outside Topeka and, although she reached Kansas City in time for breakfast, his schedule did not permit him to meet her until 3:00. He surprised her by bringing his new girlfriend, a bubbly girl who was studying to be a nail sculpturist; however, the girl apparently spent an inordinate amount of time at the radio station. In fact, she monopolized the conversation by describing in detail each of the recording artists who had dropped by the radio station to promote an album or a tour.

Although the woman didn't recognize any of the names, she nodded and smiled appropriately while sipping a diet soda. When she finally told the girl that she was unfamiliar with these performers, the girl expressed concern and suggested that the woman should hang out at the radio station for a couple weeks. The woman's son laughed nervously at the suggestion and said he didn't think that would be such a good idea.

After boarding her bus at 5:00, the woman looked at the page entitled Topics to Discuss in Kansas City. She decided that it was just as well that these topics hadn't been discussed because they'd probably be better as topics in a letter. She changed the title on the page and then turned back to her List of Stops, debating whether she should count Kansas City, MO, as #17 even though it had already been listed as #15. She decided that it, like President Grover Cleveland, should only be counted once.

Terminal

When the woman arrived in Duluth (#32) just before noon, she was worn out from too much not-doing-anything. In spite of long hours napping on the bus, she found herself nodding off while waiting for her husband. To keep herself awake, she took out her notebook and entitled a page "Highlights of My Trip"

1. *Great breakfast at Gretchen's Kitchen in Memphis*

2.

The woman stared at the "2." while her eyelids drooped. She awoke with a jolt when the notebook slipped from her fingers and fell onto her foot. She took a deep breath, got up, and dragged her suitcases out of the terminal.

In the glare of the noon sun, the sidewalks of Grand Avenue were bustling. The cold air was invigorating after the closeness of the bus station, and she closed her eyes as she inhaled the city. How many miles had she come only to find herself inhaling the scent of Birmingham, of burgers grilling and people kicking up the day's dust?

But there was another scent in the breeze that swept down Grand, something that floated under and around the other scents, something the woman didn't yet recognize. It was Lake Superior, a few miles to the northeast, saturating the city with its history and its hopes.

The woman's reverie was punctured by the insistent bleating of a car horn, and she saw her husband waving frantically at her from the driver's side of an unfamiliar vehicle. She walked toward him with her head tilted as if unable to understand what been waiting she was seeing.

"It's our new SUV," her husband shouted, sliding the back door open for her suitcases. "Get in before we get a ticket."

The woman clambered obediently into the back and sat down as quickly as possible, looking around the vehicle as her husband slid the door shut and hurried away from the curb.

"Where have you been?" he asked. "I've for half an hour at least."

She wrinkled her brow. "I've been inside. Why didn't you come in?"

"Why didn't you come out?" he said. "I said AT the bus station, not IN the bus station."

In silence, the woman began a list in her mind:

What I Should Have Said

Why didn't you just say 'Meet me outside the bus station'?
Why didn't you say that you'd be at the curb in your new SUV?
Why didn't you park somewhere and take me to lunch?
Why didn't we meet at a restaurant?
Why didn't we meet IN a restaurant?

Finally she asked, "Can we stop somewhere for lunch?"

"No can do, hon," he said. "Got a sales meeting this afternoon. You'll have to fend for yourself at the house."

He dropped her and her suitcases at the edge of the driveway behind the house and was gone before she'd walked to the back door. As she reached for the knob, she realized that he hadn't given her a key. She twisted the knob hopefully, but it refused to budge.

She zipped her jacket and walked toward a weeping willow beside the lake. A flock of geese honked above her, and she wanted to honk back, wanted to go with them, wanted to be back in Birmingham more than anything she could think of, and knew that she'd soon be gathering her wishes into a list.

§ § §

KR Mullin holds a BS in Biology, an MA in English, and an Italian Greyhound in thunderstorms.

He wrote his first short story in 1950, his first poem in 1955, and his first bad check in 1971.

If offspring could choose their parents, KR Mullin would be the child of Geoffrey Chaucer and Emily Dickinson. He can be reached at <u>krm6343@yahoo.com</u>.

THE SLIPPER

by J.P.W

All that is left behind is a fine slipper made, impossibly, of glass. (A mistake, folklorists - learned people - say. A mistake, it was meant to be mouse fur. The softest of mouse fur, gray; in the movie it is singing mice who save her. Not glass.)

You know this tale. You've heard it in a thousand shapes and forms, how her mother was dead, her step-mother a monster; how she slaved in the ashes escaping from the fire. How she hid her beauty behind a mask of grime and soot, like those moths whose wings shift color to match their surroundings, for camouflage.

You've heard it a thousand times: the cruel step mother, the dead father, the two ugly stepsisters (who were afflicted more by the ugliness in their souls than that of their appearance, though after a moment with each the Prince saw no difference; they don't tell that).

They always tell about the slipper, how it went from softest mouse fur to fragile glass. How it gleamed on the steps after she had gone, cold and austere and silent.

When it was lifted the glass caught shadow and light both like captured smoke wings of caged birds. When it was held in his hands the light slid down the clear contours of sharp, pure glass like a star, no different from the hundreds of other stars, suddenly drawing attention to its lovely pale fire.

Once upon a time. You've heard the beginning.

And the clock struck midnight. You know the end. Maybe they had been dancing or talking; it doesn't matter, because she runs. All that she leaves is a slipper made of fine, breakable glass.

The Prince went to each and every household, looking for

the girl whose foot fit the slipper. You know that too: how one of the sisters cut off her heel, the other cut off her big toe, cramming over-sized feet into the shoe, desperate. Glass is meant to be pure, clear: the blood slid like oil off water from its surface, poured out when the Prince was afraid that the sisters' blood had clouded the secret held in glass forever.

The secret held in glass forever: that is what he thought would happen. That is what he thought, until the shy, dirty girl with a tangled mop of hair walked out of the room like a shadow and he noticed her.

And once he noticed her it was like magick at work. Except it wasn't magick at all. She said to the harsh music of her stepsister's laughter, in a voice like the delicate tangles of ash and soot and soft gray fur floating in the air from her fires:

"Let me try the slipper."

And they were married in great estate. You'll hear from some stories that she forgives her stepsisters, who drop down on their knees and beg, sincerely sorry for all those slaps across the face just because they'd felt like slapping somebody, for all those times they mocked her hair, her hem singed by cinders, and the name. Cinder. Maid. Servant. Slut. (You'll maybe notice that they were sorry only because they were caught.)

You'll hear that on the day of the wedding each sister waited outside the church door to beg forgiveness, that the birds pecked out their eyes with hard, wet red beaks.

And they lived happily ever after.

And that's when the story ends, except it doesn't.

What you might hear is how this story is about negative transformations. That all girls expect a prince to walk into their living room, sit on the love seat near their parents while their little sibling looks on, holding a slipper made of glass in his hand. How the prince only loved her because she wore fine and fancy clothes, because she had the slipper made of glass, because she was skin beautiful instead of deeper than skin. How there are no such things as fairy Godmothers and history is cruel to pass this story down, because hope is unbearable when captured in unattainable expectations. Because hope is unbearable when it is gone, like the boyfriend or rock idol you were obsessed with. How girls should not try to be something they are not and girls should not think that happiness lies that way. Cinderella Complex. There's an entire book about it.

And I don't know about any of that. It might be true.

But there's something that they forget to tell, lying by omission.

They forget that she walked into that ballroom which was filled with all the eyes of the kingdom and great ladies and great lords who wore their riches and perfumes from palaces in the Arabian Nights. That she was alone. They see only the gown, of stars, the slippers, of glass, the crown, of tears, the skin, so fine, the eyes, so clear, the throat, bared, the poise, so lovely, the beauty, her gown which dazzles. The unbreakable glass slippers which lend her a grace beyond her own. (Because she must step lightly, or else. In another tale maybe her grace would feel like she's walking on knives or like each step might break the glass and transform it: let's talk about negative transformations.)

That's what they all saw, even her jealous sisters: the fine, fine lady.

But she felt like she was in somebody else's clothes when she paused in the door at the stop of the stairs and looked down at the dancers. They did not fit her: too fine, too grand, too far from who she was herself, and naked. Imagine her fidgeting with her fan or her sleeve or her skirt, a luxury of cloth she'd never had. Looking at her pale, clean fingers and uncomfortable in somebody else's skin. Wanting to find a place to sit out of the way and watch her night of dreams spin by.

The Prince, perhaps bored amid all this splendor, his life,

saw that the clothes didn't fit, that she was uncomfortable.

And he asked her to dance anyway.

Moral: "If you put a peacock feather on a sparrow the sparrow is still a sparrow."

§ § §

J.P.W. is a would-be bard who had a crush on Ffleweddur Fflam when she was a little girl. She is a college student somewhere in California, and it looks as though she will be one for quite some time.

To e-mail her use heliosradiant@hotmail.com

WHY MY HIP GAVE OUT

by Vincent Peloso

Because I was under the influence of an illegal drug,
not paying attention to what I was doing
although I was doing it for the first time
when my hip gave out.

Because the vacuum cleaner I was trying to move
was a new purchase, awkward and heavy.
Unfamiliar with how best to maneuver it, I
did not account for its unequally weighted components
so my hip gave out.

Because the space I was trying to fit the machine into
was so tight, it only fit one way.
I had not yet figured this out
when my hip gave out.

Because the vacuum itself had been so filthy
from the store reselling it used and uncleaned
of dog hair, flea powder and dead fleas,
we had actually talked of bringing it back
but didn't because I had already cleaned out the mess
when my hip gave out.

Because I had received a massage the day before
from a new masseuse using a hard foam bolster
under my chest. This dropped my hips
as she pressed into trigger points where
my hip then gave out.

Because this injury is near where I hurt myself
lifting a piece of concrete

less than five years ago,
and now my hip gives out.

Because I recently tore a calf muscle
on the same side as this hip
which now gave out.

Because years ago a calcium deposit
on my Achilles tendon, again on the same side,
caused me a lot of pain
before my hip gave out.

Because I was fighting an outbreak of genital herpes
chronically not getting adequate sleep,
ignoring the stress encountered at work
and still recovering from my father's last visit,
his first since my mother died.

Because it would soon be the first anniversary
of my mother's death.

Because my sex life is problematic,
and this depresses me.

Because one of my students acts like she has a crush on me,
and I am trying to respond in an appropriate manner.

Because my hips have always been stiff,
tight and inflexible, probably the result
of trying to exit my mother's womb sideways
before the doctor reached in
and turned me around.

Because I am fifty years old
yet failed to do any stretching before
I started to vacuum.

Because one of our cats again peed on the floor,
and I have just discovered this.

Because the country I am a citizen of
is again at war.

Because I had just revised a poem
about lying to protect myself.

Because my hips hold me up, help me move, jump and
dance,
and I have always been a poor dancer
since the girl across the street
slapped me for picking her up
while dancing in the seventh grade.

Because my hips connect my head to my feet,
my thoughts to my steps, my words to my walk,
leaves to roots, heart to crotch, brain to whatever
is under there, all that is not cerebral:
shadow, brother, life on this earth,
memory's cradle, sexuality's nest, love's mysterious
basement,
the floor below the heart's foul shop: the shelf
where the seed sack is kept: hip
joint, socket, pivot and flex: rock
and roll's groove, Hippocratic, hypnotize, hippocampus,
hypotenuse, hippie, hop, hope, help and pop
is the sound I heard
when my hip gave out.

13 Hand Held Remote Control Devices on a Glass Topped Coffee Table

by Vincent Peloso

One for the overhead lights.
One for the ceiling fan.
One for this room's thermostat connected to the central air-conditioning unit.
One for the drapes across the sliding glass door overlooking the lake.
One for the curtain hanging before the floor-to-ceiling wall mounted screen.
One for the overhead video projector hanging from the ceiling.
One for the amplifier on its custom built shelf open to the closet behind it.
One for the multi-compact disc player on the next shelf down.
One for the video cassette recorder on the shelf below that.
One for the DVD player next to the VCR.
One for the dual automatic reverse audio cassette deck hardly ever used.
One for the stereo AM/FM tuner used even less.
And finally one master remote capable of doing what all the rest do if only we knew how it works.

§ § §

Vincent Peloso lives in Arcata, California, works at the College of the Redwoods and for the past nine years has hosted The Mad River Anthlogy, a twice-monthly poetry program on KHSU radio, 90.5 f.m.

You can reach him at vfp1@humboldt.edu ..

THE BLUE MUG

by Tamara J. Lee

Someone is leaving remnants of his life on her front patio. It starts with a blue ceramic coffee mug on the plastic table next to the wicker lawn chair. As if someone abandoned his coffee to run for the phone. She's on her way to the office when she spots the mug. Assures herself it belongs to a thoughtless neighbour. She must get after her landlord about that gate lock.

Later that night she notices a newspaper placed on the table beside the mug. She picks it up anticipating something significant. But it's just the Sports Section.

The next day, when she leaves for work, she's aware that the newspaper has been folded and placed under the mug. She hesitates, then picks up the mug, gently, and turns it over. *Otto's Transmissions*, in fine gold print, is emblazoned on one side. A barely distinguishable coffee stain grazes the inside wall. She runs a finger across the scar, still wet enough to smudge. Then she places the mug back, cinches her trench coat tighter and scuttles for the bus.

When she returns home, the mug is still there. The paper is not. A half-smoked cigarette has been blunted out in the mug. She wonders if she should wash it out, as she fumbles with her front door lock. Perhaps she should wait. Surely someone realizes his mug is missing. Surely someone is teasing her.

She laughs. Out loud. Because she knows she has to learn to laugh at herself. And she urges her laughter to sound calmer. She thinks, then, that a silent smile would have worked just as well. Maybe better, because it is more assured. Like someone who can handle anything; more like Isak Dinesen in *Out of Africa*, and less Bridget Jones.

If the mug isn't gone by the end of the week, she decides

she will wash it and put it back. Or maybe she'll keep it. She pictures herself at her kitchen table, drinking her milky tea from it, holding it with both hands, and blowing whispers over the steam.

This morning she finds another cigarette butt. This one stamped out near her doorway. The mug is gone. Sometime between the late evening and early morning, he came to retrieve his mug. She wishes she had washed it for him; she is a little ashamed, now. He might think her dirty. Perhaps he took the mug in the late evening, while she was lying in bed, reading *Justine*. If he came about 11:30, he'd have been standing there while she sucked her bottom lip in uncomfortable anticipation of Sade's nasty boys. She had put that story down several times, red-faced and perhaps more than a little moist. Has he read Henry Miller? she wonders.

She should have washed the mug. If he came in the morning, he might have been there when she woke up, or as she got out of the shower. She is conscious of her ground floor bedroom; wonders if her silhouette can be seen through the blinds. She remembers last year, comforting an hysterical neighbour lady after she saw a masked man masturbating outside her window at midnight. Could it be him? Had the masked masturbator moved on to her window? She makes a mental note to check the blinds and the lighting when she gets home. To see how much of her can be seen. And the door locks, of course. Maybe the mug has resurfaced. Maybe it is on the arm of the lawn chair, a folded up paper, perhaps the Arts Section tucked under it.

Six more hours until work is over. And then she can go home. But she has some errands first. Maybe buy a new nightie. Stop at the florist's. She bites her lip to hold back a smile.

§ § §

80

Tamara is a fiction and screenplay writer from Vancouver, BC.

She participates in a film group that has just finished their third short ("A Pencil-Thin Moustache") and she is readying the promo packs for the festival season.

This is her first published fiction.

She may be contacted by email at: tjl@excite.com.

IMPRESSIONS OF AUGUST

BY Marie Eyre

Marie Eyre writes, "I am a retired musician and published author, residing in Ontario, Canada. I have been published on the Internet, in literary journals, and in newspaper venues. My interests, outside of art and poetry, lie in the fields of Quantum Physics and UFOlogy. I have always dabbled in artistic endeavors, but with the advent of the computer & 'digital art' I feel as if I have finally found my medium. I believe that art must resonate to inner senses & not end with the eye. I thoroughly enjoy impressionism, especially when the artistic message is enhanced rather than shrouded." Contact her at poetsinger@excite.com

TRASH DAY

by Beverly Carol Lucey

I get up, remember it is rubbish day and decide that if I can just throw out the trash I can get clear and get going. That's how it starts.

I feel a little bored, just a little restless. The night before I had this little thought that the everydayness of being middle-aged, being known, being expected to be in the same old places by people who expected me to just jump to it at certain predictable times was curling around me like the tendrils of those grape vines choking my day lilies out front. I never pretended to be a gardener.

It looks rather ordinary to anyone out walking a dog, I suppose. I bring out the bags and bags of food wrappers, take out cartons, and general junk that piles up over a week, put it on the correct side of the driveway, then go back for the recyclables. I lug the cans in one bag, glass and paper in their separate brown bags just the way the new town policy reads. Underneath the stairs I find a stash of newspapers crushed behind a big Coleman cooler. The old headlines seemed so important at the time, but the world has moved on to newer outrages and political embarrassments by now, so I stop worrying about old news and drag that spider webbed shopping bag full of papers outside, adding it to the others.

Next I decide there must be lots of stuff in that old cellar that we'll never use so I start piling up broken beach chairs, empty paint buckets, two leaky rubber rafts, rusted tools. No one has revved up that chain saw in years, or the band saw. Wooden cross-country skis are a pain, what with the different colored waxes and all. Bye, bye, long useless sticks and poles.

I toss in a dog carrying case, a broken bike, boxes of books.

And then I just keep going...our new skis, my husband's weight bench, exercycler, his new mountain bike, all the garden tools, a huge glass jar of chutney I made one sweaty August, and an industrial strength wet-dry vacuum cleaner.

The driveway is getting crowded and people stop to ask if this is a tag sale. I say it surely is and go back through the cellar up into the house and start bringing out all my kitchen stuff. I take pictures off the wall, bring out all the lamps. Cars stop and one lady, apparently trying to help, begins to tell people how much things are. She starts collecting money for me in one of the baskets I picked up during an auction at Bilodeau's in South Deerfield years ago. I had tossed it on the pile at her feet a minute before.

The phone rings while I am loading the boxes from the pantry into bigger boxes so I unplug the phone and add it to the pile.

People begin to ask for things: "Got any records?" "Got any cloisonne?" "Got any brass or copper?" "Keys?" I invite them in. They get some good bargains, let me tell you. The two marble-topped tables are gone before I turn around.

Around three o'clock it is all over. The house is pretty well empty, upstairs and down. In my bedroom I find a canvas bag way in the back of my closet. Two volunteers from the local Homeless Center have followed me and stand around while I pack three days worth of stuff. I leave them opening drawers and go on down stairs. I yell up over my shoulder that they can have at the rest...both sides of the closet, husbands's stuff too, yes, surely. That helpful lady with my basket gives me a wad of bills that I figure I'll count out later. She says she had a great time and she loves the owl print I let her pick out for free. The trashmen come, swear really loud in case I can hear them, and take what is left.

The refrigerator is empty because of the thirsty, hungry helpers and a couple of customers, but I put the one Lean Cuisine Chicken Parmesan left behind in the freezer out on the counter with a note:

Supper in a box. No other boxes left.

I'm off,

Me

BY THE NUMBERS

by Beverly Carol Lucey

"Five words," he said. "It's all you get."

"I need more."

"Sorry. You just used up three. Better make the next two count."

Bon closed her eyes so Raleigh wouldn't see how much she hated him. She wondered if there was a two-word key she could use to set free the man from this monster of madness that had taken over.

Raleigh's medication had floated out of his pocket five days earlier when their canoe tipped over. The ten-day wilderness trip brought them too far from anywhere to save either of them. Unless she could come up with two good words.

Remember when

Marco Island

The kids

Our plans

Your book.

Finally Bon tried out loud,

"Love me?"

"No. Good try. But maybe it will hurt less this way," Raleigh whispered as he slowly ran the sharpened knife along her calf, in the first of many delicate slices.

GLASS HOUSE

by Beverly Carol Lucey

As it turns out, the sound of breaking glass isn't just one sound. I don't pay attention, I guess. Or, at least, not enough. Otherwise, I wouldn't have stood at the sink using my Scrubber-on-a stick to orchestrate how that damn blue jay went after our puppy this morning.

I should have stayed at the table, talking to my husband after supper, tamping up crumbs from the blueberry cake with my index finger, then used the finger to do the blue jay swoop and peck. That way, the half empty bottle of brandy on the counter I had dusted off around noon before macerating the peaches for the neighborhood brunch this weekend wouldn't have taken a swan dive onto the tile floor making a heavy splitting sticky sound. Four big pieces and the dusky smell of Armagnac is not a catastrophe. I should have put it away when I was done. I know that. But I didn't.

I should have worn shoes while cleaning it all up, but then I hate shoes and never wear them in the house. If he hadn't yelled at me from the den, "You're going to hurt yourself," while I was backing up, holding the four pieces carefully out in front of me, reaching for that paper bag I'd jammed under the blender a few days ago, I wouldn't have jumped and my elbow wouldn't have met with the carafe of the coffee maker.

94

I should have realized that the explosive yet soft sound was a sharp silica version of a chrysanthemum firework blooming at my feet, but I couldn't just stand there.

He'd already told me once, twice, a downright host of times, that I was on my own regarding danger. He said, "You are too careless. I can't stand to watch you. I will take you to the hospital when the worst things happen, but you will get no sympathy from me." Since he hadn't seen this part yet, I figured I could very quietly reach down and get the dust pan without moving much.

Right now, the sound of glass is like crushed ice. If only it were cold it might numb my feet which are bleeding a little (not too much yet) but at least I am alone in the kitchen and can take care of it myself.

The sound of glass being swept up into a dustpan is like the muffled skitter of bug carcasses and nail clippings. My back and arms shiver and goosebump, as if the wind has picked up, but it's only me in my tiny chaos. By now I've shoved my red sticky feet into my rubber garden shoes so he won't see the tracks I've made if he comes back in the room too soon for a snack.

I don't mind so much when things break. So far, it's never been a chandelier on my head, or the spear of an icicle thwunking from the roof turning me into a brain kebob.

The sound of glass being sucked up into a small canister vacuum cleaner reminds me of the uneven pinging of tumbling gems I saw once when a lapidary explained how he made sharp stones soft and and silky and warm, easy to touch. He gave me a rounded rock that fit my palm perfectly. He called it my harmony stone.

I can picture my husband in the den, white hot and furious over the loss of the brandy (VSOP and a gift from his brother), flicking from station to station as though the remote were a magic fire stick. He is sure I am a threat to organized society, the society in which one must always take care, and be wary of possible threat. I think it is harder to be him.

At last, it looks as though everything in the kitchen is pretty much back in order. I've tweezed a few shards from my right foot pad. Ting, ting, into the bucket. The lavender ointment I keep at hand feels soft and cool. If I hold my breath, there isn't one sound around me.

§ § §

Originally from New England, Beverly Carol Lucey writes now from the Land of Lard and Peaches.

Four stories are anthologized in We Teach Them All *(Stenhouse Press, Maine) Two slices are in the 1999 edition of* The Flint River Review; *"Birthday Tape" is in the winter 2000 print edition of* Moxie. *"Worry Circuit" appeared in the Spring Edition (33) of* Quality Women's Fiction, *2001 (UK) Wild Strawberries ('03)*

Her online presence is getting fat: Zoetrope All Story Extra has published: "Gift Wrap" (July 2000) "Scissors, Paper, Rock"(January 2001); "Waiting for the Flight," flash fiction in Vestal Review,was nominated for a Pushcart Prize. (2001) Other work can be found at CollectedStories.com, flashquake, and the winter edition ('03) of Would That It Were.

She lives with her husband and black standard poodles, the elegant Miss Bessie Smith and the slightly trashy Lillian deLuna. They are adapting to a suburb outside of Little Rock, AR, after five years in GA.

LAWRENCE FERLINGHETTI

Fragments from an Interview
by Ernest Beyl

I met poet Lawrence Ferlinghetti in December 2001 at City Lights, his landmark San Francisco bookstore at 261 Columbus Avenue. In the 1950s, City Lights was a veritable clubhouse for writers of the Beat Generation. Today, it's a magnet for baby-boomer tourists and their offspring who read Ferlinghetti and Beat Generation writers like Jack Kerouac, Allen Ginsberg, and others. City Lights celebrates its 50th anniversary this year.

I was at City Lights to interview Ferlinghetti for a book I'm writing about San Francisco and, well aware of his towering reputation, I was apprehensive about talking to him.

Ferlinghetti is widely recognized as one of this country's greatest living poets. This is the man -- not actually a Beat poet himself -- who published Allen Ginsberg's epic "Howl," a poem that became a Beat anthem. "Howl" was deemed obscene by the San Francisco Police Department, but Ferlinghetti vigorously defended his right to publish it, as did noted defense attorney Jake Ehrlich, and, after a much-publicized trial, the San Francisco Municipal Court ruled in favor of Ferlinghetti. The judge's opinion: "In considering material claimed to be obscene, it is well to remember the motto: honi soit qui mal y pense (shame to him who thinks evil thoughts.)"

These days, the poet, painter, pamphleteer, former Poet

Laureate of San Francisco, publisher, and bookstore proprietor strides through the streets of San Francisco's North Beach like a colossus and continues to rail at big government, big business, civil rights abuses, and this country's pugnacious war stance, as he always has. At 84, he walks tall and straight, his pale blue eyes fixed on another orbit. He has a mesmerizing presence.

Once I was seated in his wedge-shaped, manuscript-cluttered office above the bookshop, this is how that interview went:

LF: Where is your tape recorder?

EB: I'm sorry. I suppose I should have brought it.

LF: This would work better with a tape recorder.

EB: I'll bring one next time.

LF: I don't have much time.

EB: Let's meet again and I'll bring my tape recorder. Meanwhile, let's talk for awhile.

Ferlinghetti shrugs purposively. He looks doubtful about this meeting.

EB: Can we discuss the role of poetry in society as you see it?

LF: Do you mean the roll (r-o-l-l) or role (r-o-l-e)? The poet's role is not to roll over. Get it? The poet's role is to exhort and harangue and to defend our civil rights. Our civil rights are constantly being challenged. They are being eroded daily.

A series of long vertical panels draped along the façade of City Lights Booksellers and Publishers read: "Dissent Does Not Mean You Are Un-American." And: "Stop War and War Makers."

EB: Actually, what is the state of the poet in our society?

LF: The usual.

EB: I take it you mean by "the usual" that most people only read poetry once in awhile or don't read it at all.

LF: Poetry and poets are on the sidelines. If you have the time, it's okay to read Byron, maybe Shelley or Keats, but not a bunch of crazies.

EB: Well, who does read poetry these days?

LF: Almost everything is threatened and repressed. In our colleges and universities, all the professors talk about is, "What is the process of poetry?" They don't ask what it means. I give poetry readings at colleges and the idea of the readings is to get the listener HIGH. Oral poetry, which is just one kind of poetry, should get people HIGH. But everyone wants to know about the process; how you wrote something. No one cares about the content, just the process.

EB: Well, who reads poetry besides the poets themselves?

LF: Maybe a token poet who is a professor; or a token professor who is a poet.

EB: Today, what other kinds of poetry are there besides oral poetry?

LF: There is documentary poetry. I am working on a documentary poem now called "Americus." It's modeled on Ezra Pound's "Cantos."

EB: What do you think your legacy will be?

LF: That's up to the professors to decide, if they are interested in the question at all. They are in the deep sleep of the well-fed.

EB: There's a common idea that you are a Beat poet and were a member of the Beat Generation.

LF: Of course not. I was a member of the last Bohemian Generation. I even wore a beret. I published the Beats. I published Allen Ginsberg until later when he went over to Harper and Row. By that time he had shot his bolt. Did you get that? He shot his bolt by that time.

EB: Let's not dwell on the Beats, but rather on some other ideas and opinions, about the community in which you live. What's good about it; what needs improvement?

LF: Next time bring your tape recorder.

EB: Okay, I'll do that.

I rise to leave.

LF: Sit down and read this.

He hands me The Argonaut, a publication of the California Historical Society.

EB: I was going to leave because you said you didn't have much time. I'll bring my tape recorder next time.

LF: Sit down and read this.

The fall 2001 issue of The Argonaut features a profile of Lawrence Ferlinghetti. We sit silently as I read the entire, five-page profile.

EB: You seem to be a very public person, yet also a very private one. Since what I plan here is a profile on you, what are you comfortable in telling me about your personal life?

LF: Nothing.

EB: I knew you were going to say that.

LF: Who's Who sent me a questionnaire once to fill out about my life and I wrote across it "fuck you." They sent me another questionnaire. This time I thought I would give them a surrealistic answer. At that time I thought I was a surrealistic poet. So I wrote, "I was born either in 1919 or 1920. Born either in Paris or New York, etc."

We sit and look at each other for a few minutes. I have run

out of gas. I stand and am ready to make my exit.

EB: Thanks. I appreciate your time. Next time I'll bring my tape recorder.

LF: Sit down.

Ferlinghetti reaches back into a cubby hole of the roll-top desk at which he is sitting and brings out what appears to be a greeting card. He turns to the desk, takes up a pen, and writes on the card.

LF: Here, this is for you.

The single-fold, black-and-white card depicts Rembrandt's 1655 drawing, "Abraham's Sacrifice." It shows an angel, one hand over Isaac's eyes, the other restraining Abraham from killing Isaac. Below the illustration Ferlinghetti has written "By Rembrandt and Ferlinghetti." In a cartoon bubble coming from the angel's mouth he has written, "If you can't look him in the eye you can't kill him!"

I open the card. On the left panel he has written, "Happy New Year!" On the right panel he has written, "To the bombers who kill thousands from 20,000 feet. Lawrence Ferlinghetti, 10, December, 01."

What makes Ferlinghetti a great poet is not only his work, but his unshakable belief in the importance of the poetic voice and his confidence that poetry is capable of transforming the world. He's viewed by many as an urban guerilla at the barricades. Critic Karl Malkoff (Crowell's Handbook to Contemporary American Poetry, Crowell, 1973) describes him as a man whose work is "built around the tension between the poet's wish to participate in some greater unity, some wholeness that can survive the prevalent fragmentation he sees all around him, and his need to participate in deadly events of his time, his need to confront the dark heart of experience rather than turn away from it."

In his monumental "A Coney Island of the Mind," published in 1958, he writes about an urban environment in which

101

he was able to bridge the gap between being a passive but visionary poet and an active poet of radical defiance:

Who may cause the lips
of those who are asleep
to speak

And in the same poem he
tackles just what it means to
be poet:

Constantly risking absurdity and death
whenever he performs above the heads of his audience
the poet like an acrobat climbs on rime
to a high wire of his own making

§ § §

Ernest Beyl is a San Francisco writer currently working on a book about the city called "Why I Live in San Francisco." It is not a guidebook but rather a series of essays on San Francisco people, places, and pleasures. Chapters from the book appear monthly in the Nob Hill Gazette as work in progress.

He also has contributed essays to Saveur, Westways, and the North Beach Beat. A poem titled "Gongman" has appeared in the North Beach Journal. He is a former newspaper reporter, Hollywood press agent, and U.S. Marine. He lives on Telegraph Hill and plays the Chinese gong for the Green Street Mortuary Marching Band. He may be reached at:beyl@earthlink.net ..

THE SLIGHTEST BETRAYAL

by Richard Hollins

The phone creaked in his hand. Martin relaxed his grip and pressed the handset less tightly to his ear. With more time, he would have mapped out his approach, shopped around, at least composed an opening speech for this call. His wife's imminent return had wrong-footed him. In less than seventeen hours, Audrey and his children would be home.

Just as he was about to abandon hope, the woman picked up. There was a brief delay before she said, "Hello," and her breath echoed in the mouthpiece, loud and sleep-dazed. It was five pm.

"Hello?" she said. This time it was more interrogative. As Martin started to speak, he had no firm idea how far he would go.

"Hi," he said. "Could you tell me a little about yourself? What you look like? How old you are?"

"Sure," she said. She was brighter now, businesslike. Her voice was plummy, like a second-rate American actor straining for an English accent. "I'm twenty-three," she said, "five six, slim but curvy, and a genuine blonde." Martin visualized her mouth's exaggerated shapes as she formed the words; from time to time, a south London dissonance broke through. Even so, her apparent intelligence surprised him.

"You sound nice," Martin said. He adjusted what this woman had told him - five years on her age, two inches off her height, the exact volume and placement of her body fat - and decided she was acceptable. He hoped her blondeness was not too obviously fake. "What's your availability like?" he said. "Tonight?"

There was a pause. "I can fit you in around nine," she said. "Where?"

From his window, Martin could see a stream of descending planes. He had a clear mental picture of this woman's place, an anonymous, pebble-dashed thirties semi, split into two apartments. Between here and Heathrow were street after street of these houses. Outside the flat he imagined abandoned cars, and inside, a faded gold velour sofa, on a carpet with ancient, inexplicable stains. Once, Martin had attributed a perverse glamour to these estates; they were authentic in a way his own upbringing was not. Now, he would not pretend to feel safe there. "Can you come here?" he said, and gave her the address. Martin was no fool: he would watch her every second she was in the house.

"That's fine," she said. Then almost as an afterthought, she added, "Cash only. And with a condom. No exceptions."

"Of course," Martin said, though he felt vaguely let down. Not by her demands - he expected nothing less - but by the suddenness of her puncturing their air of pretence. "Can I ask your name?" he said.

"DeeAnne," she replied.

"Tonight, then, *DeeAnne,*" he said, and he put down the receiver.

The house around him was silent, except for the fridge and the clock counting seconds in the dining room. . Martin closed his eyes and rested his index fingers on his lips, hands together as if praying.

The call pleased him. His underarms were damp and cold but he had carried it through and not laughed at her name. DeeAnne! He doubted there was a woman in England called that. It reminded him of the topless models in the tabloids - Rebekkah from Essex, Linnzi from Manchester - teenagers hoping for something better, their ordinariness exposed by implausible spellings. Martin understood that these working girls had to disguise themselves. Four newsagents traded on the main street's half-mile, and in each of their windows, he had found the same three handwritten cards. He had rejected the *Genuinely Friendly*

Lady, seeing her as fiftyish, motherly. He had declined the *VIP Escort*, with her grainy photocopy in stockings and underwear, as too open to the deal's true nature. In any case, he doubted the picture's provenance. That left the last card. Three things drew him to *Luxury Discreet Massage*: the notion, however spurious, that the service was deluxe; the correct spelling of *discreet*, suggesting the author knew its meaning; and the telephone number, the only one not a mobile. Somehow, this grounding in the physical world seemed safer. That was the number Martin had dialed when he got home.

At eight pm, he showered. It took twice as long as usual. He dried himself and slapped talc on the places he tended to sweat. A smattering of white powder outlined his curled-in toes on the bathroom floor. As he reached for his underwear, the phone rang. He took the call in the bedroom. He had not heard from Audrey in forty-two days; now she had phoned twice in four hours.

"There, are things," she said, "that I need you to know." And she talked while he stood there, naked and chilled in the October evening. She was still coming back, that hadn't changed. But if it was going to work, they had to be honest. "Don't get upset," she said. "Let's not get emotional. But your personality flaws just drive me insane. Lord knows, I've said this before, but the fear in you! You're too scared to leave that bloodsucking job, too scared to tell your mother to screw herself, too scared - my God - to take a holiday in *France*. My blood pressure is *off* the scale. And before you say anything, I *never* claimed to be perfect. *I* admit that I can do better.

"At the very least," she said, "we should try for the kids. They need two parents. And, for what it's worth, I love you. Every time I roll over in bed and you're not there, it *hurts*."

"It's been hard for me, too," Martin said, "without all of you."

"Can you change?" she said. "For me? For us?"

"I'm trying right now," he replied. And he was. Martin was being less timid and tackling life head on. And although

Audrey could never know about this evening, it was sufficient that he did. He would hold it inside himself, a pearl soothing away Audrey's irritating anger. He tucked the phone between his ear and shoulder and began to dress.

Audrey talked on. While she did, Martin thought about his other reason for phoning DeeAnne.

At nine pm, the doorbell rang.

"I have to go," Martin said. "My pizza's here. I can't wait to see you three tomorrow."

Audrey was silent. Then she said, "Are we going to be okay? Is this the right thing?"

"Of course," Martin said, "of course. I love you." Then, he hung up.

DeeAnne was not quite what he had envisaged. Her height and body were as she had claimed, and while her blade-like, slightly twisted nose left her just short of pretty, she was pleasant enough. Her hair, though, was a harsh straw yellow. The short, swept back style suggested a Hollywood star a few years before, though Martin could not remember her name. Several chemically destroyed strands leapt at bizarre angles from DeeAnne's head.

"Come in," Martin said, "please." He stepped aside and allowed DeeAnne to pass. He closed the door, then turned to face her. She smiled, displaying her gums and haphazard teeth no bigger than Tic Tacs.

"Where do you want me?" she said.

"Upstairs," Martin replied. "First door on the right." He swallowed, then coughed, failing to shift a sudden dryness in his throat. With a wave of his hand, he indicated that DeeAnne should lead the way. Her clothes - a pinstriped trouser suit and snug white t-shirt - fitted around and into her curves. Their cut was passable; their effect was brisk and professional. Her strappy black shoes had three-inch heels, tapering to a metal tip. Martin had never understood

106

the allure of such footwear, but he had to acknowledge that she knew how to walk in them. As she climbed the stairs, DeeAnne's buttocks moved like bearings in oil, a hint of exaggeration in their lateral shift. Martin wondered why Audrey disdained these sexual tricks; women who used them appreciated their worth. DeeAnne reached the top of the stairs and Martin directed her into the bedroom. She stood by the bed, waiting for his next move. Martin yanked the curtains shut. Then he switched on the overhead light and the lamp on Audrey's side of the bed.

"Would you like me to undress?" she said. Martin nodded. DeeAnne bent and fiddled with her straps, kicking off the right shoe, then the left. Then, staring into the middle distance, she stripped. She could have been preparing for a shower after a rough day at work. But it had been such a long time since Martin had seen another woman naked, that the artlessness of DeeAnne's disrobing failed to perturb him. The fact of it was enough.

When Audrey first left, Martin had expected her back in a week. But as the house's silence closed in, he began to doubt she would return. Her mother protected her, taking her in, screening her calls, refusing Martin's entreaties. Twice he spoke to Tabitha, who was too miserable to assess her mummy's state of mind. The third Saturday, Martin planned an offensive on Audrey's bolthole. He took the train to Dorset. But in a taxi on the outskirts of Lyme Regis, unable to confront the massed female righteousness allied against him, he lost his nerve. On the trek back to Waterloo, the idea crept in that his marriage was through. And on the service out to his southwestern suburb, the train full of drunks and an air of low menace, a second idea arrived: his next sexual experience would be with someone new. This notion took root. The only problem was finding an available woman. Pubs and clubs did not suit him, and the few women he saw - strolling by the Thames on Sundays or perched on high stools in coffee shops - had an impregnable aura of self-sufficiency or damage. Anticipation became Martin's sole pleasure. Who would it be? What would she look like? How would she smell, feel, taste? He explored the permutations in his mind. He thought about this woman and how they would find each other. So when Audrey did call, beneath Martin's relief was unqualified fury: this, too, she was tugging from his grasp.

He had not allowed that to happen.

Martin examined DeeAnne, the way he might an ambiguous sculpture with no obvious way in. She stood there as if waiting for a bus, confident of her physique. Martin could not remember the last time Audrey had let him admire her.

He thought of his wife. He thought of Tabitha and Toby. He thought of how he had felt when he knew they were coming home. He told himself this was a small thing, the slightest betrayal.

"How would you like me?" DeeAnne said. And though Martin knew instinctively what she should do next, he was still amazed when the words came out of his mouth. In his experience, there was nothing harder than asking for what you desired.

"On the bed," he said, "please. On your hands and knees."

"That," DeeAnne said, "costs extra."

Martin counted out twenties until DeeAnne nodded. Then he overturned the wastebasket and sat on it, opposite the bed.

DeeAnne fished a condom from her bag and dropped it on the bed. Then she arranged herself. Martin suggested she put her weight on her elbows. From directly behind, he could not see her head. The woman on the bed could be anyone: a mistress, a girlfriend from Martin's pre-Audrey days, even his wife, if he squinted.

Martin leaned forward. He slipped from his seat and knelt at the bed's foot. It was incredible, he thought, what was available if you reached out and took.

"What are you doing?" DeeAnne said. The pillows muffled her voice. She lifted her head.

"Get down," Martin said. "Don't move."

DeeAnne hesitated, then pressed her face into the pillows. Martin saw her breathing accelerate. He held his breath, then exhaled slowly through his nose. The condom sat in front of him. He moved his hand towards it and ran his finger along the rough-edged square packet. He gripped one corner of the packet in his teeth and ripped it open. A bitter drop of lubricant hit his tongue. He ran the taste round his mouth, as he regarded the woman with her face buried in his wife's pillows, on the bedding his wife had chosen, in the room his wife had decorated.

"What are you doing?" DeeAnne said.

The pillows did not disguise the bright edge of concern in her voice. Martin noted the tremor in her thighs, as the bitterness filled his mouth completely. He turned away from DeeAnne and slumped back on the carpet.

"Thank you," he said. "That's enough."

DeeAnne bounced from the bed and crouched to retrieve her clothes from the floor. She tugged on her underwear; while her t-shirt was still half way over her head, she began edging to the door.

Martin handed over an extra five twenties.

"I'm sorry," he said, "if I scared you." DeeAnne snatched up the money. But she did not glance at him as she strode down the stairs and across the hall to the front door. She slammed the door behind her.

* * *

From the living room window, Martin watched his wife parking the car in the street. She maneuvered the vehicle in small, precise increments, though she had plenty of space. He opened the front door. Tabitha was already out of the car and had her arms spread wide as she ran down the path, childish joy on her face.

"Daddy!" she said, and she wrapped herself round him. Her foalish limbs dug into his sides and Martin cupped her face in his palms.

"Hey, sweetheart," he said. "I missed you. Did you miss me?"

Tabitha released him and took a step back.

"I *hated* it at Grandma's," she said.

"I know what you mean," Martin replied. He glanced up and saw his wife at the gate. Toby, their three year-old, was slung on her hip. The boy seemed bemused.

"Come on you two," Audrey said. "Grandma does her best." Her tone was mock serious but she was smiling with one side of her face.

"Hi," Martin said.

Audrey stepped up to him and Martin took Toby from her. He hugged his son and smelled his hair. Then he lowered Toby to the ground. Martin and Audrey embraced. Then they kissed, and the contented noise she made at the back of her throat told Martin that they were all right. He was glad that nothing had happened. He was the world's worst liar, the most inept deceiver. Audrey would have pried it out of him in five seconds flat.

They let go.

The children had already entered the house and Audrey looked past Martin into the hallway. Her eyes narrowed. Then she said, "Darling, what on earth have you done to the floor?"

"Where?" Martin said. He turned round and saw the floor's glossy maple surface, the crescent dent where he had dropped a coffee mug when the floor was one week old, and the six-foot groove where Tabitha had dragged a box of old baby toys. And he saw something he had not previously noticed, to do with the angle at which the light hit the floor and the damage's newness: punched into the maple were two distinct trails of half-moons. One trail meandered from the door to the hall's edge, then led straight to the stairs. The second ran from the stairs to the door, the impressions in the wood like craters.

"Oh," Martin said. "That." There were words, somewhere, that would extract him from this mess. He did not know what they were. He looked at his wife, an enquiring smile turning up the corner of her mouth, and began to speak.

§ § §

Richard Hollins lives and works in London, England. His fiction has appeared in print magazines in the UK and in on-line journals such as Eclectica, Small Spiral Notebook and In Posse Review.

He is currently studying for an MA in Creative Writing and working on a novel. He can be reached at richard.hollins@talk21.com.

SHAKESPEARE DISCARDED

by Michelle Cameron

Flinging me aside
like last year's fashions,
she says she tires of my sighs,
my whispers, my importuning,
my sonnets,
my love.

Her laugh a silvery tinkle,
now cold and clanging,
freezing the blood
that still throbs
and pools at the sight
of her.

She tells me our passion
was never more than dalliance,
smiles through rouged lips
that I -- yokel, hireling,
ink-stained lackey --
might aspire to more
than a few privileged nights.

I see her, putting that small hand
through Southampton's arm
as he leads her to dance.

I want to close my eyes,
blot out sight of her -- and him.
But, somehow, my lids refuse me,
become fiery prongs of torture,
making me watch,
unblinking, red-rimmed,
seared.

§ § §

Michelle Cameron's poetry has appeared or is forthcoming
in several electronic publications, including *Riding the
Meridian; 2River View; Samsara Quarterly; Stirring; The
Paumanok Review; jerseyworks;* and *flashquake.* Print and
anthology credits include poetry in *Lilith; LIPS; Uno;
Midnight Mind;* and *The Paterson Literary Review.*

Her poems were selected as "Editor's Choice" in the 2002
Allen Ginsberg Contest, and Best of Stirring Year Three.

Michelle's first full-length book of poetry, "In the Shadow of
the Globe" will be published by Lit Pot Press, Inc. in
December, 2003, as part of the Literary Potpourri Poetry
Series.

She lives in New Jersey with her husband and two sons,
and has a day job as Creative Director for an Internet
company. More of Michelle's work can be seen on her web
site at <u>http://www.noretreat.org/mec/</u>

SHEEP SHE SAYS

by Kay Sexton

'Sheep,' she says, 'are so underrated. That one's Tess ...of the D'Urbervilles, you know?'

'Ha ha,' I say. Tess stares. I stare back.

'Yes...,' she says, 'we have three sheep, lawn-mowers, you know, for the grounds?'

'What else could they be for?' I think, 'the carpets?' But I say nothing and she babbles, she is brittle, social, unable to let dislike have its silent way.

'It's our little bit of heritage,' she says, 'preserving rural ways.'

I look back at the ranch-style house, double-garage and pool. 'Of course,' I say.

I grew up here, within ten miles of the "little bit of heritage". It was just a field on a farm, unnamed except by whatever the farmer called it to distinguish from all the fields. Now there are six ranches (double-garage and pool) where one farmer, his family and two labourers wrestled with the seasons. My dad worked on the farm: I remember silage clamps and the farmer's new Land Rover next to our collapsing Morris Minor. I went into electronics.

'Claggy bottom,' I say.

'Sorry?' she says. She's not apologising, just regretting that I'm here. Bizarrely, she sees me as an urban creature, unable to 'do' rural. She's half right.

Her husband's business and mine are linked. It's like Tess and the 'grounds,' we're mutually necessary, but we don't bother having feelings for each other. That's her department, establishing the right feelings to have about me. They'll be something like, " ... such a deep young man, hard to get close to, but brilliant," or "He's a wonderful businessman but he needs to focus on something cultural, he's rather ... well ... socially inept." Whatever she decides, it will settle me in my place, like Tess, who must on the right side of the fence, in the grounds, not on the manicured garden or in the chemical blue pond.

'If blowflies lay eggs around sheep's arses, they develop claggy bottom. Best to find out now who'll come in and deal with it.'

'The vet, of course,' she snaps. She's reconsidering my urban status, but downgrading me in her social standings. I try to conceal a smirk.

'Doubt it,' I say, 'there's no farm vets left around here, only small animal practices.' I should know, my sister works in one. 'You could put her in the MPV and take her to town, but the maggots drop everywhere. You'd have to valet it afterwards: the car, not the sheep.'

We stare at Tess.

'You can do it yourself,' I suggest. 'You just need shears, dip, gloves and some tweezers for the deep burrowers.' I lean towards her, watching her head retract. She hates me, and Tess is heading down the popularity stakes too. I offer her my wisdom, hard-earned. 'After the first couple, it's routine, like knitting.'

She turns and goes back into the house. Tess and I stare at each other.

§ § §

Kay Sexton is a published writer who spent two years as an agony aunt for nudists - it was an education, although for what is not clear.

FANTASIA DELL'ARTISTA

by David Allio

c2003 David Allio

c2003 David Allio

119

About the Artist

David Allio is an international award-winning photographer and photojournalist whose professional portfolio ranges from fine art and portraiture to sports, corporate, glamour and fashion work. Since 1974, his images have appeared on album covers, billboards, display advertising, and in movies, books, catalogs, calendars, magazines and other periodicals.

This second generation Italian-American's fine art figure nude images have been exhibited in museums, art galleries and private shows throughout the United States, in Japan, Australia, New Zealand and several European countries. Original Limited Edition Prints and Commissioned Works by Allio are prized by private collectors worldwide.

An online gallery of Allio's images may be viewed at: http://www.davidallio.com

BABYSITTING

by Pia Z. Ehrhardt

Greg was watching Sherry's niece, Kai, get dressed through the half-opened door. He thought Sherry was out running errands, so he peeked as Kai buttoned her blouse, put on lipstick, crunched her hair with her hands to mess it.

"Busted," Sherry said, startling him.

"Oh. Hey there," he said.

"Lecherous behavior, Gregory. Some countries would cut off your dick."

Kai was living with them in New Orleans for the summer, after Sherry's sister, Erica found drugs in her backpack. She'd just finished the eleventh grade. Sherry liked the idea of her niece filling the place up. She wanted her to know how she and Greg lived. He worked at an art gallery, and Sherry produced documentaries for the public TV station in town. They were both forty, had been together since college, and Kai was fresh air.

Sherry closed the door. "First time you've done this?" she asked.

"No," he said.

"Eighth time?" She knew the answer. She didn't want to admit that she spied on her, too, like a guy, *just one touch, please, and I'll know what I can't have.*

Now Greg was afraid to get too close to Kai. He sat on the other side of the room, and didn't make eye contact.

Kai's father was Polynesian and her mother, Italian. She had a wide face with tawny skin, light eyes, and full lips she stained pink. Her name meant sea in Hawaiian.

"He's acting weird," Kai said to Sherry. "You two having

trouble?" She went to take a shower.

"Act normal," Sherry told Greg. "You look shifty and weird."

"No," he said. "I'm making coffee." He set out the cups and saucers, put cookies on a plate.

"You're wearing slippers," she said, looking at his feet.

He kicked them off and went barefoot. Sherry slid her feet into them and skated around. He almost smiled. She didn't tell Greg she'd like to be the one parading herself in front of a guy she thought was kind of old, a little dull, nice.

"I'm courting a child," he said.

"That's sick," Sherry said.

"I know. It feels rotten."

"Liar."

"Yeah, it feels great."

Sherry sat at the table and peeled an orange. "We have to return her."

"When?" he said.

Kai walked in freshly showered with her hair in a towel turban.

"Not yet," Sherry whispered. She wanted to keep Kai, steal her away from her sister, change who she loved like a mother, like she tried to do when she was sixteen and babysitting people's kids. Libby Turner's parents had taken her with them on vacation. Sherry had worked hard to win Libby's love - tea parties, paper dolls, nature walks - until the child wanted only Sherry. She sat on the other bed while Libby slept, a guard against the monsters but different than a parent, her private friend.

Kai came out in shorts and a tank top and her legs were long and smooth.

124

"Let's sit on the balcony so your hair dries," Sherry said.

It was as tiny out there as everything else in the apartment with room for two wrought iron chairs, a small table, and one potted plant. Their place overlooked the cupola on top of The Napoleon House. A pigeon was standing on a weather vane of a chicken.

"Do you want a little glass of wine?" Sherry asked, and Kai nodded a big yes.

They chatted. Sherry asked her questions, treated Kai like she was an expert witness so she would tell her what it felt like to sneak out of the house at 3 a.m. and screw her boyfriend at the boat launch under the night sky, riggings clanking in the wind.

Sherry was working on a documentary about the Mississippi River, and she took Kai to work. She wanted to show off her pretty niece. Kevin, the cameraman, came over and asked Kai how things were going. He wanted to know how old she was; he guessed twenty-three. Kai liked him right away. It hit Sherry like a brick in the face that this was a bad idea. When Kai ran for Cokes and snacks, the gaffers and grips watched her and exchanged looks. She wanted to fire them on the spot. She was a thousand miles away from not her own youth, but Kai's, and all that sloppy allure that came from not caring completely about what you had, what you did, because there was so much time left, a big wide life of anything's possible.

Kevin set up an orange crate so Kai had a place to sit. The day was long. Kai was happy, helpful. By the time they wrapped, she knew everyone. She stood on the crate, braiding Kevin's hair. "You better get her out of here," he warned Sherry. "I'm in love."

Erica, called in the morning to see how it was going. "My kid driving you crazy yet?" she said.

Sherry was straightening up, folding Kai's afghan in half

and the phone was between her shoulder and chin. "She's great. Easy." Her underwear was on the coffee table, socks and shoes were beside the couch. "She's hamster messy, though. You didn't tell me that."

Kai walked in with Greg, and Sherry told her sister she had to go. He held bags of pastry and the Sunday paper and Kai had a paper cone of red tulips.

"Where'd you go?" Sherry asked.

"Tower Records," Greg said. "We had a fight."

They stood in front of Sherry and told their sides. Greg wouldn't let her buy Mystikal. Kai said she listened to gangster rap all the time. Greg said not on his watch.

Kai put the flowers on the table, went into their room and closed the door.

Sherry followed her. "I'm not a kiddie," Kai says. "The parental advisory sticker is for *him*."

Sherry lay across the bed. Dust outlined the blades of the ceiling fan. If she used the feather duster junk would fall on her head. "He hasn't been around teenagers much," she said. She was selling Greg out to win Kai back.

"I bought the CD anyway," Kai said, "while he was buying the flowers." She went to her suitcase, which had stuff spilling out of it, and dug for a doll sized sweater.

"Can I try on your clothes?" Sherry said.

"Sure." Kai found another little sweater and some baggy jeans. "Here."

Sherry stripped down to her underwear.

"You look good for your age," Kai said.

"I'll accept pity." Sherry pulled on the jeans. They were too big and fell around her hips, so she hitched them up.

"Leave them," Kai said. "You want to show skin."

Sherry wrestled the sweater over her head and tried to tug it down. She could feel the air on the band of skin.

She walked out to the living room to show Greg, and he smiled big and grabbed her waist. His hands were warm and she held them there like compresses.

Greg was reading the paper, and Kai came up behind him and asked if he wanted a head massage, and he said okay.

"Your scalp's tight," she said. "Open your mouth wide as you can, then relax." He did. "Close your eyes tight, then relax." He did. "Your hair's warm. Are you blushing?" she said, and looked around at him like she was peeking behind a corner. She looked over at Sherry and said, "What is it with guys?"

"You tell me," Sherry said.

At dinner, they were running out of things to talk about. Kai's interest in them was looking like good posture. Sherry didn't want to lose her to the same dullness she probably felt with her mother, so she looked up Kevin's number, called and asked if he'd drive Kai around. Kevin said sure and thanked her like she'd given him a gift. Kai left the table to get ready. Sherry told him to have her back by eleven.

She and Greg stood around the bathroom door and listened. The noises lined up so pretty - radio, shower, the quiet toweling pause, hair dryer, zippers, perfume sprayed. Sherry rested her head against the doorframe, and Greg had his hands in his pockets.

Once, when Sherry was babysitting for the Harrington's, the little girl complained about an itch, and Sherry had her lie down on the bathmat. She'd never seen her own genitalia, didn't know it was so ugly and beautiful. She had washed the child with a warm cloth, and washed her again.

127

"Did I take too long?" Kai said, when she came out. The bathroom was all steam and roses. Sherry went in and rubbed a spot on the mirror, but it was only her face.

With Kai out, Greg and Sherry sat in the living room and looked at the walls. Greg put his head back and closed his eyes.

"Would you have sex with a seventeen year old?" Sherry said.

"No."

"Eighteen?"

"I don't think so." He was breathing slowly and didn't open his eyes.

"What can I do to make you feel like that?" she asked.

He ran his hand through his hair. "I don't want to feel like that with you."

Sherry went into Kai's bag and dug through her clothes. She found a gauzy shirt with embroidery on the sleeves, and she took off her blouse and bra and put it on and went back to Greg. "Don't do that," he said.

"This is for me," Sherry said.

They made love, and it was a full bed, combinations of Kai, Kevin, and this older couple who had fucked eight hundred times plus this.

Sherry thought about the children, the ones she'd wooed and won, who didn't remember her anymore. All of that work for what? She had bumped into one of the families, the Barclay's, at the mall, and the young boy shook her hand and ran off to play in the arcade. The thought of having her own kids frightened her, the day in and day out when she wasn't the fun-machine, just the mother, how dangerous is was to be a parent.

It was a cool night. The French doors were open and a

woman with a thin voice was singing. Tourists were under their balcony, and the guide was telling them a ghost story.

Erica called to talk to Kai, and Sherry lied and told her she was at the movies with the daughter of a friend.

"Is she going out with any guys?" Erica asked.

"No," Sherry said. "She's mostly here with us. This is her first night away."

"That's strange."

Sherry told her everything was fine and Kai would talk to her in the morning, but Erica wanted to be called when she got home.

"Why?" Sherry said.

"Because I can't sleep when she's out."

"Pretend you don't know."

"It doesn't work like that," Erica said.

"We'll call in the morning," and Sherry hung up.

The wind was blowing out of the north and the shutters were banging, so Greg hooked them open. The moon was bright and in that homely phase. They ate ice cream out of the carton and watched TV, fell asleep on the sofa during the news.

Kai walked in two hours late.

"Where were you?" Sherry said, half asleep and confused. Greg got up and said he was going to bed.

Kai was swaying in the door. "Just driving."

"Drinking?"

"Beer on the levee. Kevin showed me the elevators where

they store rice."

Sherry eyed her and for a second couldn't remember whether she was talking to a roommate or a niece. Sometimes when she babysat she'd forget there were children in the house. One night at the Winstead's she got stoned and went to pick up Chinese food while the twins slept. "You're playing me," she said.

Kai stared her down. "No. I'm not."

Sherry wanted to slap her into being sorry. "I was worried sick," she said.

"Really?" Kai laughed. "I think you're exaggerating, aren't you?"

Sherry shrugged her shoulders and agreed because she wanted to know about her night. Every detail. What part of her Kevin touched first, her hair, how the streetlight hit collarbones, bare knees, if she brushed his cheek with her fingers, if they made love under that ugly moon. She lowered her voice to a secret. "My mother used to say that, too, when I'd come in late, but I didn't care because I was with some guy so good I didn't need a home."

"Yeah, he's that."

"So, how far did you two go?"

Kai looked at her in amazement and laughed. "Uh, let's see . . . I let him steal home."

"I'm supposed to be looking out for you," Sherry said.

"I'm fine," Kai yawned. "Probably time for bed, don't you think?"

Sherry went to the hall closet and got the sheets to make up the couch.

"I can do that," Kai said.

"No problem."

130

Kai watched her, impatient.

"Are you having a good time here?" Sherry said.

Kai shoved her hands into the pockets of her low jeans. "You guys are great. But I'm okay with going home, too, and getting back to normal."

"We'll miss you," Sherry said.

"I know. My mom and I worry about you and Greg," Kai said. "We wonder why you don't get your own kid."

"Really?" Sherry said. "Tell your mother it isn't a kid that I want."

It was Kai's last week in New Orleans, and they went to dinner at an Italian restaurant on Bienville. Greg ordered veal shank for four, a giant bowl of angel hair, and a bottle of red wine. Kai touched his hand and asked if he wanted to split an order of bruschetta and he said sure.

Kai's long hair was pulled back except for two skinny braids that hung down the sides of her face and touched the table. Kevin picked one up and looked at it more closely. He'd dressed nicely for her in a laundered shirt, khaki pants, and his hair was clean and loose.

He and Kai chattered about bands and TV shows. She looked lovely in the candlelight. Her shirt had a bright pattern on the front, and a different pattern on the sleeves. Kevin held her hand.

Sherry asked Greg about his day, and they talked and tried to pay attention to each other, but they would've preferred sitting in a dark theater watching Kai and Kevin.

Sherry touched Kevin's knee with hers under the table, but he thought it was a mistake and apologized. "Are you happy with the footage?" he asked Sherry.

"It looks fine," she said.

Kai leaned over and put her arm around Greg's neck, squeezing him in the bend of her elbow. "This is mine in ten years," she said. Greg looked happy at the thought, took her hand from around him and cupped it in both of his, like a bird was in there.

That night in bed, Greg said how different the apartment was going to feel without Kai. Sherry asked him if he was in love with her, and he said a little. She wanted him to not be. Sherry told him how she babysat once for a widower with kids. Mr. Kleinschmidt. Her boyfriend came over and they drank the man's vodka, sat naked on his sofa and made fun of his Sinatra tapes. It was great to live in his house like that, to eat from his fridge and fuck in his bed. The man drove her home and she asked about his night like she was the dead wife, and he told her all about it. Didn't he know she half-cared? He chattered on, trusting a teenager. When he got to her house she kept looking at him, still listening, and he kissed her. He smelled like a father and she pushed him away. She wanted Greg to know this. How the man apologized. He overpaid her, then drove off too fast. He called her to baby sit again, but she lied about other plans.

Greg was half-listening. He stared through the window at rooftops, as if Kai had now moved outside to dance for him on the tile shingles. "She's everywhere," he said.

§ § §

Pia Ehrhardt lives in New Orleans with her husband and son. Her short stories have been published in the Mississippi Review, Gingko Tree Review, Monkey Bicycle, Wild Strawberries, Pindeldyboz, and Word Riot, and she won the Fictionline.com prize earlier this year. She's writing a novel called (at the moment) "In the Driveway."

GUITARRA PORTUGUESA

by Michael Spring

in the cafe
Paredes held the Portuguese
guitar -- walnut wood -- the body
of Lisbon -- with twelve strings
his fingers emulated rain

across the room a woman began
dancing --
the fingerpicking and figueto
described her movements --
the underwater sway
of sea grass --
I was submerged

her figure haunted every glass
of water or wine

her shadow drifted through the welter
of candlelight
on the adobe walls

after the final chord
floated across the room
and Peredes put his guitar down

I breathed in deeply
the steam of baked salmon
buttery spinach and garlic bread--
the music had entered everything

I placed a grape between my teeth
tasted the dark surge of juices

when I realized I could no longer see
the dancer
I wondered if she had disappeared
inside of me

§ § §

*Michael Spring is the co-editor of Riven Poetry Journal.
His own poems have been published in over 200 national
and international publications, most recently in: Atlanta
Review, Poems Niederngasse, sidereality, Midwest
Quarterly, Verse Libre Quarterly, Pedestal Magazine,
Pierian Springs, Stirring, Sulphur River Literary Review,
among others.*

*His first full-length book of poetry, "blue crow," was just
published by Lit Pot Press, Inc. in August 2003 as part of
the Literary Potpourri Poetry series.*

*Michael currently works in Corvallis, Oregon, where he
assists mentally and physically disabled adults.*

You can reach him at Bluecrow04@cs.com .

FISHES IN THE SKY

by Jan Steckel

David is afraid of the surf at first. His parents run him into it, laughing, this is the Ocean! When it reaches for his ankles, he screams -- it wants to kill him! He flies back up to the beach towels. Though his older sister Rachel jeers, he won't be coaxed. Look, says his father, at the fishes in the waves. David comes a little nearer. Can you see them, myriad and black? A little more, sidling cautiously. There! Minnows swarm like summer gnats. They are slim black fingers. Shall I catch some for you? Oh yes. His father fills the yellow plastic pail with sea-water. Soon it is full of darting minnows and carried home.

The garden hose makes prickles in David's skin, driving all the grit off. His mother towels him and Rachel down and gives them American cheese and orange juice to hold them until dinner. He slip-slaps around in new flap-jacks, not minding the rubber thong cutting between his toes. Slap! Slap! He folds his cheese in origami patterns and slaps onto the back porch to look into the pail.

A black body floats slack on the surface while its fellows squirm beneath. Daddy, *(pointing)*, What's wrong with that one? Father says it must be dead and explains the fishly need for aerated sea-water. David insists they take the fish back now. Dinner is cooking, however, and the beach is far away. He cries and screams. Dinner is served, but he won't eat. One by one the small fish die, till not a one is left.

*****

David dreams about a new gadget, a mechanical roller with a scroll of paper on it. As he turns a knob pictures come out. First little fish swim up and down the paper strip. Then out come amphibians puffing pouches at their throats and pushing paddled feet through the water. He laughs and keeps turning the knob. The amphibians turn

135

into dinosaurs crawling up from the slime. A dragon rears its snorting nostrils -- with a start he awakes. Rachel is breathing heavily through her nose across the room. A few seconds later the space-heater breaks into its comforting hum. Then asleep. Now awake. He looks up. Over his bed, where the gray window light intersects the red glow of the heater, a fish is swimming in the air.

Quickly he turns his head away and stares at the pillow. In the wrinkles of the pillowcase, there the little fish swim. He grabs his teddy bear and holds him against the wall, and looks at him hard. There. For a moment he sees only the bear and the gray-white wall. But behind the bear's head, like a slide projection, he soon perceives the silhouette of a man standing on a pier's end, arms akimbo, with waves lapping at the pilings beneath. David calls his mother, once, twice, and finally she comes.

He tells her what he has seen, and she comforts him. No matter. Look what we'll do. She pushes his bed over next to Rachel's. There now. Whasamatter, Rachel murmurs. Go back to sleep, whispers his mother, and bends to kiss her. Sleep tight. She kisses David, and leaves the door ajar.

There are three kinds of light in the room now: gray through the window, red out of the heater, and yellow from the hall. David looks over at Rachel and sees a fishbowl sitting on her head, with goldfish swimming round and round in it. He is partly afraid of them, and partly afraid they might die. If the bowl should fall and break...

Rachel!

Mmm?

There's a fish tank on your head.

I'll knock it off, she mutters drowsily. She passes her hand over her head, and it goes right through the fishbowl, goldfish and all.

Mo-o-o-o-o-o-o-o-m!!!

******

(Gina): When you were a kid, didn't you ever make sand-castles on the beach?

(David): Yes.

(Gina): -- did you ever get handfuls of what looked like those tiny colored beads you buy in hobby shops?

(David): I think so.

(Gina): Those were grunion eggs! When the tide is highest, three nights out of three months, that's when they run. The waves wash them up in the dark, male and female. They flip-flop up the beach and slap around until they bump into each other. She bores her tail into the sand and lays her eggs, then he lets loose all over them. All that flapping around covers the eggs back up, and the surf pulls the grunion back into the midnight sea., the flashing bits of silver as every wave goes down! Unless we catch them, like we're going to do tonight! Nets are illegal, and so's a dredge. You catch them with your hands. Otherwise they'd all get scooped up at the moment of ecstasy and there'd be the end of the breed. Actually, *(voice lowering),* catching them at all's illegal now, but I know a place. They're a delicacy. You can eat them with their heads on, they're so little, and their bones just crunch. We'll sift them in piles like pieces of eight -- and a royal fish-fry in the morning!

Laughter ripples up and down the dark beach, over the plash-plash of bare feet and the slapping of the bucketed grunion. David's jeans are rolled up to his knees, and he carries a silver flashlight. Low in the southeastern sky the yellow moon hangs brilliant. Moonlight sparks the whitecaps far, far out, but northward high bluffs shade the beach. Guardian cliffs curve toward Point Dume, enclosing sand like the crook of an arm. Into this crook, this inner elbow, safe from the gaudy lunar light, the trusting grunion swim.

The others flit from fish to fish, but David stands amazed.

Incredulous joy rises in him, and he strains to contain it. Here is fragmented beauty in a thousand silver flashes on the sand. Feeling as if he is in a dream, he raises his light and passes it over the water's receding edge. There! He starts to run toward a glimmer momentarily fixed in the beam. A new excitement vibrates through him. He stoops, squats and shoots a hand out -- gotcha! His victory shout switches to one of alarm as the fish squirms in his grasp. He tightens his hold on the slippery, jerking, beautiful thing. As he does so, a liquid line of tiny colored beads streams from the fish's underbelly, falling at his feet. He holds the fish out from him against the sky. Throw -- this -- in a bucket?

He cannot stem the upward flow of pure revulsion from his center, into a sour and watery mouth. He opens his fingers; an inch of water swirls the fish away as he retches into the surf. He vomits and coughs, drawing a ring of baffled faces. He straightens, finally, and in shame rebuffs concern. Yes, I'm all right. He pushes past, fleeing unsteadily Gina's proffered arm.

He stumbles back to the empty cars that wait on the edge of the sand. Sitting down on a bumper, he cradles his head in his hands. Between the booming of each wave faint cries and laughter blow up from the beach. At irregular intervals his stomach heaves. Under the twisting bodies of the captured, sperm mingles futilely with a million eggs in the bottoms of a dozen buckets.

*****

(Rachel): When I was a kid (tapping down a cigarette) we lived in a two-story house, with all kinds of pictures hung along the wall of the stairs. Pictures of me and my brother in Santa Claus's lap and pictures we made, mixed in with brass rubbings and a lot of tacky prints. My little brother David and I used to knock the pictures every which way by accident when we'd come tearing down the stairs. (A lighter flashes.) Thanks. (Two puffs.) There was this linoleum block on the wall that David had carved in nursery school. It was hung by one little hole punched in the center of its back, over a single nail, so it could spin pretty freely. The carving was of a couple of stylized fish with a wavy line over their heads -- you know how kids draw water -- and a radial sun shining down from the upper right-hand corner. One time I passed it and saw that one of us had knocked it upside-down. You wouldn't notice right off because it was all one gray and the line of the water -- *(she leans forward to tap the ashes off her cigarette into a potted fern)* -- was right in the middle, so it didn't look much different upside-down. I reached out to turn it around -- but then I stopped, and left it the way it was. *(Smiling)* Because, you see, there was something very nice about fishes in the sky and the sun shining up from the sea.

§ § §

JAN STECKEL is an Oakland, California writer and a Harvard- and Yale-trained pediatrician. Her fiction, creative nonfiction and poetry have appeared in the print and web journals Hospital Physician, Yale Medicine, Problem Child and Awakened Woman, among others, as well as in the anthologies Becoming Doctors (Student Doctors Press) and WomanPrayers (HarperSF).

Bilingual in Spanish and English, she served as a Peace Corps volunteer in the Dominican Republic before taking care of Latino children as a pediatrician first within the California public health system and later in a large HMO. You can read more of her work and contact her through her web site at http://www.jansteckel.com.

YUCATAN

by Allen McGill

We sail from Cozumel in the darkness of the early hours.
Javier, the boatman, has much less enthusiasm than I, but
agrees when the mordida, or bribe, reaches the right
amount. He carries a kerosene lantern to light our way
across the rocks to his wooden boat.

Doubts intrude when I see how truly black the sea is
beyond the lamp, and imagine the treacherous coral
jutting upward just below the surface. We push off with
only the flickering yellow from a lamp on deck, and paddle
until Javier deems it safe to start the motor.

a single flame
deepens the darkness
the wooden hull creaks

I doze, lulled by the rocking motion, awakened by the
sudden silence and a nudge from Javier. He motions west.

Tulum! The white temple glows pink as the first rays of
morning dart across the Caribbean to the Yucatan coast.
They ease into a pale yellow, then flare golden as the sun
continues to rise.

from atop a cliff
the ancients watched for dawn
waves flow silently

We gaze in wonder. Javier, a native Yucatecan, as much in

awe as I. We ease toward the shore and I jump onto the rocky beach. He passes my backpack to me, then shoves off. I turn.

Tulum is mine, if only for a short while. My time is limited. I scramble up to the temple to sit and gaze at the blue and green patterns stretching into the sunrise.

All too soon, the raucous grind of tour buses arriving breaks the silence. It's time to leave.

Beneath a palapa, hut, just outside the temple site, I collect the motor scooter I'd arranged to rent for the main portion of my trip. The old attendant looks curiously at me. I use my broken Spanish, only to learn that his is more limited than mine. Since I speak no Mayan, gestures must suffice.

jungle shade
the oldest language
unites two worlds

I head west toward the heart of the peninsula. It grows hot and humid, the road pitted and often blocked with palm branches.

Time is running short, but eventually I reach the turnoff for the ancient city, Chichén Itzá.

The Plaza of Kukulkán surrounding the Grand Pyramid is crowded with sightseers. I've arrived just in time. The hordes grow silent as the narrow strip of shade beside the steps begins to flow slowly downward from the brilliant blue sky. Quetzalcoatl, the feathered serpent god, slithers to earth once more, as he does every equinox.

as the sun peaks
its rays evoke life
I watch mesmerized

The shadow descends for hours before gradually fading away with the sunlight. The seasonal collaboration of earth and sky is complete.

142

I rush to climb the rough stone steps to the summit. The world is splayed below: jungle, plaza and the endless sky. I stand where gods once ruled.

twilight
the deep Mayan reliefs
recede in shadow

§ § §

Originally from NYC, Allen lives, writes, acts and directs theatre in Mexico. His published fiction, non-fiction, poetry, plays, etc., have appeared in print as well as on line: NY Times, The Writer, Newsday, Retrozine, Laughter Loaf, Flashquake, Herons Nest, Cenotaph, TempsLibres, Autumn Leaves, Poetic Voices, Amaze-Cinquain, Bottle Rocket, Frogpond, Modern Haiku, World Haiku Review, many others.

SCHEHERAZADE

by Andrew Nicoll

We watched the executions every day. Standing on the
terrace above my father's gate house, hidden by the
alabaster urns, we'd see the procession pass, the white
donkey driven on with blows and kicks by the donkey man
and his boy or kicking out for himself at the woman
stumbling along behind, digging her feet in, dragging her
heels, tied to his tail.

They weren't all like that. Some were dignified and upright,
pale and frightened, determined not to give in to hysteria.
But most were tearful, screamed for pity, begged for help
in the grip of shrieking terror. Nobody helped. There was
nothing to do but watch them and their howling families;
the mothers with veiled faces, the ululating aunts and
sisters,fathers and brothers weeping alongside, helpless
and ashamed. Those men couldn't save their women but
might have died trying with enough courage. That's what
they were supposed to do in this most manly man's world:
offer strength and protection in exchange for absolute
authority and the total obedience of their women. But they
never tried. They went home and beat their wives until the
shame passed.

We could see the whole street from our terrace. The
donkey used to come from behind the tamarinds on the
corner and bobbed along towards my father's house, its
sorry little procession dragging behind.

At the other end of the road, they stopped in the square by
the well. Doves crowded in the branches of the fig tree for
a better view and my sisters and I hung from the terrace,
jostling the geranium urns to see the women die.

There was an hour-glass feeling in those moments. All the
life rushed out of the victim and yet I tingled with it, blood
singing in my ears, surging through me.

In my memory all the executions were the same. For me, the killings in the square were like puppet shows from the fair - but they were all too real for those girls. Even the shriekers grew quiet by the time they reached the square and the donkey man forced them to their knees.

By then they knew their pleading was wasted, their fathers would not save them, the executioner would not look away and allow them to escape, nothing could be bargained, nothing could be given. So they knelt, hoping for the waking jolt from a nightmare, as the donkey man tied his scarf around their eyes and walked back to his donkey and pulled that long, thin, glittering blade from under the blanket.

The donkey man stepped forward, dancing lightly, silent on slippered feet in the dust, graceful like a falling hawk, quick paces, one step, the sword went back, two steps the sword was still, three steps, the donkey man's boy touched the woman on her shoulder with his stick, she started, sat bolt upright, the blade swooped forward, sliced through her neck, head fell, side-step, four steps.

The doves in the fig tree took flight at the rush of it and circled round the square, landing on the rooftops, cooing while the blood seeped out in thick pools on the pavement. When the body was taken, wrapped in its white shroud, with a weeping father leading the way to the fresh grave, the donkey boy would scour the slabs around the well, bucket after bucket bobbing up and down on its pole and spilling over the square, chasing the blood down our street.

And then he washed the donkey and made its white coat shine and fed it carrots; he brushed and garlanded it under heaps of knotted roses and put daisies behind its ears and an embroidered riding cloth over its back. After that we watched the second procession of the day when the donkey man went to a new victim's house and escorted her to the palace to be married to the Sultan for a night. We heard the shawms and the tambours and her family's howling as they walked behind the band, scattering petals in her path.

After the first month of these rituals, the women of the town stopped using the well at the end of our street and went to the one on the other side of the fruit market. It was further away and the water was heavy to carry but they said it was worth it. They said our well had a taste to it.

By that time my sisters and I had long ago stopped watching the executions. They were boring. The same story every day. A poor sort of play this when the story never changes. We heard the weeping and the scouring at dawn and the weeping and the music at noon and the weeping and the scouring at dawn but we seldom looked out from our house.

That was how my father liked it anyway. The neighbours hated him because he was the Sultan's vizier but they would have fired the house if they had known of his crop of daughters behind the gate, laughing and singing like waterfalls, swaying like palms to the sound of lutes. Father kept the gates locked and the screens drawn.

But one day the donkey man came. He had been to the neighbour on the left and he had been to the neighbour on the right and now he came to our gate. My father had given orders that we should open to none. But the donkey man stood all day at the gate and knocked and he was still there at evening when my father returned from the palace.

Father cursed him. Father denied there was any woman in the house. Father came through our gate, pale and ashamed and said that, the next day, at noon, the donkey man would lead a wedding party to the Sultan's palace. My sisters wept, my father wept. They were all afraid but I was not afraid.

I was glad. My father could not choose my older sister because she was his first child and he had loved her the longest and he could not choose my younger sister because she was but a baby and he could not choose me because, above all things, he loved me the best. But I offered myself.

I demanded that I should be the one to go and, while they spent the night in tears and argument - for we all loved one another and each of my sisters would have given their lives gladly for the other - I went upstairs and dressed myself as a bride.

The next morning we heard the procession go by with weeping to the square at the well and the blood ran red past our open gate. And then at noon the white donkey came, covered in roses with its embroidered saddle cloth and I mounted and rode to the palace with my father and my sisters walking on ahead, throwing petals and howling as if to drown out the musicians in front of us.

By my marriage I became a queen. With modest eyes I gazed at the Sultan over my veil during the wedding feast and I saw that he was beautiful and I felt my body open to him and I longed for him - whatever might be the price. The endless meal ended and, at last, I was brought to the Sultan's chamber where I cast away my veil and let him look on my face and I knew that he was enchanted and, when I danced for him, he was captivated. He reached out to me but I floated away, the silk clinging to my body, the shape of me left shimmering in the air and he growled.

"I have been married many, many times" he muttered in his beard,"and even if I could have remembered their names, I never asked them. But tell me yours."

I danced close and whispered "Scheherazade" with a tiny, tinny clash of my finger cymbals in his ear and danced away again with just the scent of my perfume for him to hold.

How he wanted me then. And he wanted me more when I sang to him and poured his wine until he was drowsy and kissed him, long and deep and talked to him and told him stories. I told him of the poor orphan boy, Aladdin, and the wicked sorcerer who lowered him into a cave of treasure and the magic lamp and the genie who dwelt within. I told him of the brave sailor, Sinbad, and the bottomless gorge, scattered with diamonds and how he was lifted out of it into the sky in the talons of the great Roc. Such wonderful stories I told him until dawn. But I would not give myself to him.

148

In the morning, when the donkey man came to the door, the Sultan shooed him away - as I knew he would. There was no reason to kill me. My fingers had found the mound in the Sultan's trousers. That had not been there for the others. He need not kill me to hide his shame.

But he was tired and he sent me away to the empty harem where the morning peacocks were screeching on the lawns and gold fish flashed in fountains of lapis mosaic. There the eunuchs, those great fleshy capons who giggled when I tickled them and twittered like birds when I danced, served me. Pleasure without danger. I shook my buttocks for them, I teased them with my fingers, I worked them with my mouth and soon they blossomed and they had me, each of them, one after another until I quivered with pleasure and moaned with delight. Yes, it was disloyal, but as deadly a secret for them as for me and I have needs as well as a brain.

That evening, the Queen of a second day, I went back to the Sultan and danced and sang and teased and told stories. I told him of a Prince who saw his kingdom stolen by a wicked uncle and a faithless mother, driven to murder by his father's ghost. I told him of a man who wandered from farm to farm with his giant friend in search of work - and killed him for love. I told him of a worthless man who found himself a place in Heaven when he gave himself up to death for another - for the love of the other's wife. But I would not give myself to him.

Again, in the morning, the donkey man came to the door and, again, the Sultan sent him away and withdrew, burning, to his bed, while I retired to the empty harem and my peacocks and my gold fish and my fountains and my eager eunuchs.

And then, on the third night, I told him of the struggle between a fat man and a man with a pointed face and how they battled for a golden falcon, studded with jewels. I told him of a man whose niece was stolen by savages and how he searched through the desert and the snows that he might kill her to save his name but, at the end, his love was too great and he let her live. And I told him of men who sailed to the moon sitting on the top of a great rocket

149

as high as the Grand Mosque and fell back to crash softly in the sea bringing nothing but moondust with them.

The stories never ended and, all the time I touched him and stroked him and kissed him and pleased him but, though my want was as hot as the desert winds, I did not let him have me. His want grew for a thousand nights and a night and mine was slaked in the harem every morning.

Until, at last, the Queen of a Thousand Nights and Two Nights, as I played my lips and tongue over him again, he admitted it. "I have loved you from the first, Scheherazade. No woman has ever pleased me as you have done. No woman has your charm, no woman has your beauty, no woman has your peach arse. Then I knew that he and I were a pair and our love would last unto the grave and I would lie beside him as his Queen forever. For Scheherazade is no woman and never was and the mound in the Sultan's trousers is not quite as big as the mound in mine.

§ § §

Andrew Nicoll is 41, married with three children and lives in a tall Victorian house by the beach on the east coast of Scotland. His first published poem appeared in Lit Pot last year. Short stories have appeared in In Posse Review and Paumanok Review. Further poetry will be anthologised in a print publication The Pagan Muse later this year.

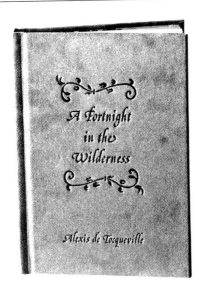

A Fortnight in the Wilderness by **Alexis de Tocqueville** $39.95
(# RB0740) available October 1, 2003

Forthnight in the Wilderness is from the diary that Tocqueville kept in preparation for the great book, Democracy in America, as he travelled through America in 1831. His wilderness began in Saginaw, Michigan. He writes of the mysterious Indians and the majestic forests, both even then disappearing.

We commissioned the Michigan artist Judy Finnegan to bring Tocqueville's vivid descriptions alive through watercolors. Then we bound our 5 1/4" x 7 1/4" hardcover in soft, green suede and adorned it with copper foil lettering. Its 102 pages are printed in two colors on a cream paper.

A Fortnight in the Wilderness is a provocative account of the country we once were and the people we still are. What does it mean to be an American? Remarkably, part of the answer still lies in this 172-year-old journey.

STAFF

INDEX